TREES
OF BRITAIN AND EUROPE

■ FIELD ■

NATURALIST'S

■ LIBRARY ■

TREES
OF BRITAIN AND EUROPE

BOB GIBBONS

INTRODUCED BY

TONY SOPER

WHSMITH

EXCLUSIVE
· BOOKS ·

This edition produced exclusively for
W H Smith

Published in 1991 by Hamlyn Publishing Group Limited,
part of Reed International Books,
Michelin House,
81 Fulham Road,
London SW3 6RB

ISBN 0-600-57082-7

Produced by Mandarin Offset

Printed and bound in Hong Kong

Colour artwork by Ian Garrard, Tim Hayward, David More and Roger Gorringe, first
published in the *Hamlyn Guide to Trees of Britain and Europe*

Contents

Introduction by Tony Soper

There is a world of difference between a single specimen tree in park or garden, and the individual member of a great woodland community. One will be tended, pampered, pruned and given pride of place and an aura of permanence; the other must take its chance, nurtured in the shade of its elders, waiting to thrust into the light and grow to maturity.

But an oak is an oak, whether it prospers as a show specimen or an unremarkable member of a mixed woodland. Or rather a *Quercus robur* is always a *Quercus robur* – our English Oak – and that is what this book is all about. It is a guide which tells how to distinguish one tree species from another, wherever it may be growing.

The two tiny seed-leaves of a broad-leaved tree mark the beginning of a life which may span centuries. Each stage of development, from springy sapling to gnarled old giant, presents so different a picture that it is sometimes difficult to believe they represent the same plant. But each species of tree has its own signature: whether the leaves form the 'needles' of a conifer or the broad leaves of a deciduous tree. The size and shape of the leaves and the arrangement of the veins, the shape and colour of the buds and time of year when they appear, the colour and texture of the bark, the shape of the flowers, the scent... all these features, noted one by one, will point to the identification of a particular tree. It may be an easy task or a complex one which demands close examination of the hairiness of the leaves or a count of the stamens. The detailed description and illustration of each tree in this guide points the way.

Trees are such a familiar part of our everyday scene, whether we live in the leafy suburbs, town or country, that it is easy to take them for granted. But we all look at them with different eyes. The commercial forester is looking for timber, and huge plantations of softwoods are the result. The gardener has an eye for colour and variety, mixing evergreens and deciduous species to create a particular atmosphere and to provide shelter from wind or sun or the neighbours. The gardener may look for a fruit crop for himself, forked nest-sites for blackbirds, berries for the thrushes. Each will plant for different reasons and create a haphazard patchwork of growth.

In the agricultural landscape, too, trees display different shapes and sizes according to the job that is asked of them. In hedgerows, trees with enormous growth potential can be reduced to shrubby status. Or in woodland, whole stands of Hazel or Sweet Chestnut are cut to ground level to regenerate small timber from the base, for the basket maker or the hurdle maker or the craft market.

This kind of manipulation creates different growth forms to confuse the tree spotter. And natural developments like a dense coat of ivy may cloud the issue, too. So it is clear that identifying trees can be a challenge.

Over 200 species are described in the guide. Many are introductions from far away places, but their long-term familiarity has given them a sense of belonging. It is difficult to think of our landscape without Sycamore or Horse Chestnut, for example. And a feeling of permanence – even though we know they pass through stages of youth, middle age, maturity and death, just like us, is one of the attractive aspects of trees in our landscape. Individuals are marked on maps, given names, mentioned in literature and have a place in lore and legend and individual memory from the welcome shade cast on a mid-summer picnic to the sad felling of a family friend.

Because trees are all around us and so familiar – despite the fact that our natural woodlands have diminished to slight remnants – it is easy to look on them merely as 'trees'. But so much more exciting to know their names, where they come from, how big they will grow and whether they will grow at all in the water-logged soil or where it is very acid. Most people can recognize the common species, but here is a chance to pin down a great range of different trees in every kind of situation.

WHAT ARE TREES?

People often think of trees as something quite apart from ordinary flowering plants, and it often comes as a surprise to discover that trees have flowers at all. In fact, the term trees is not a term like 'ferns', 'mosses' or 'conifers' which each describes a group of closely-related plants; rather, it is a term that describes a motley collection of plants from a wide range of types of flowering plants that share certain physical characteristics. The main feature that links all trees, whether they are closely-related to lilies, foxgloves or roses, is the presence of enough woody tissue to form a distinct trunk and woody branches, at least for some of the time.

Strictly speaking, trees and shrubs are usually defined as plants in which the main stems and branches increase in length annually by the outgrowth of buds at the tips, and increase in diameter by the concentric growth of new internal layers, called secondary thickening; this virtually corresponds to the idea of them being woody, which is probably simpler to grasp. Shrubs are separated from trees in that a tree has a definite single main stem (the trunk or bole) between the roots and the crown, whereas a shrub has several or numerous stems arising at ground level, and rarely reaches more than a few metres high. For the purpose of inclusion in this book, a tree is defined as a woody plant that regularly reaches a height of three metres or more on a single stem.

In fact, it can be far from simple to separate a tree from a shrub just by looking at one example. A species that may regularly grow into a tree can often pass through a shrub stage, or occur in less-than-ideal conditions as a shrub all the time. Other habitual trees, such as Field Maple, may be managed as part of a hedge, for example, and therefore remain permanently in a shrubby condition. The two words do overlap therefore considerably, and we have only included those plants that do regularly form trees in good growing conditions.

8

The spreading crown of a mature Scots Pine, Pinus sylvestris

Types of trees

The simple general definition of a tree as being a woody plant with a single stem of more than three metres hides a multitude of different types of tree; to take two examples at the extremes of variation found within this book we have: the Giant Redwood, or Wellingtonia, *Sequoiadendron giganteum*, which is a Gymnosperm rather than a normal flowering plant; it reaches 90 metres high, with an enormous girth of many metres diameter at the base, weighing many tons in total. Another plant included as a tree is the Guelder Rose, most frequently found as a shrub about 1.5 metres high (though also occurring as a very small tree), with broad-lobed triangular leaves rather than the scale-like needles of Wellingtonia, masses of showy white flowers in heads, and a total weight of just a few pounds. The two are very different in growth form, size, weight, appearance, ecological preferences, geographical distribution, and evolutionary origins, yet both can be classed as trees! Clearly, some further subdivision is necessary.

Trees come primarily from two great classes of plants – the Gymnosperms (which includes all the conifers) and the Angiosperms, which includes all the familiar flowering plants.

The Gymnosperms have two major orders in which trees may be found – the Gingkoales and the Coniferales. In the Gingkoales, there is just one species, the Maidenhair Tree, which has leaves like those of many a common broad-leaved tree in appearance, but which shows its relationship to the conifers (albeit a rather distant relationship) by its flower and fruit structure. The Maidenhair Tree is an oddity, highly primitive in evolutionary terms, and unlike any other group.

The Coniferales are a much larger and more familiar group, including all the well-known conifers, such as pines, spruces, yews, firs and so on. Virtually all of them are evergreen (though not quite all, and quite a number of trees from other groups can be evergreen, so this is not a diagnostic feature of conifers), most have narrow scale-like leaves, and generally the seeds are borne 'naked' in dry woody cones, rather than enclosed within a fruit, as are all the seeds of the Angiosperms.

The Angiosperms include the vast majority of familiar plants, in a huge spread of variation in form, from tiny aquatic plants like duckweeds, through bulbous plants like tulips, to massive trees like beeches. The trees within the Angiosperm group are drawn from all sorts of families, with close relationships to a wide range of purely herbaceous plants. Some Angiosperm families, such as the buttercup family, have no tree representatives, whilst others, such as the willow family, or the oak family are virtually all trees or shrubs. A few families are largely herbaceous, but just have one or two trees within them, such as the foxglove/figwort family, which encompasses a huge variety of herbaceous plants, plus *Paulownia*, the Foxglove tree.

In general, the multitude of trees from the Angiosperms, such as beeches, oaks, birches, ashes and so on are known collectively as broad-leaved trees, as distinct from conifers. To the forester, they may be known respectively as hardwoods and softwoods, though the distinction is not quite so clear-cut. One further subdivision of the Angiosperms that may be made is that into the Dicotyledonous plants and the Monocotyledonous plants. The 'dicots' have 2 seed-leaves (cotyledons) contained within the seed, and they are plants that have broadish leaves with a network of veins. In contrast, the monocotyledons have a single seed-leaf, and, generally, long narrow leaves with parallel veins. The latter group includes all bulbous plants and their relatives, such as lilies, tulips, crocuses, orchids, fritillaries and so on, as well as all the grasses. They contain very few tree representatives, partly due to their different internal structure, and the only two in this book are the last two species – two palms. The remainder of the trees in this book, which are not Gymnosperms, are dicotyledons within the Angiosperm class.

To subdivide trees further – in other words, to identify them – we need to look more closely at a number of features that are used to help classify them. Some of the characters that we use are genuine taxonomic differences, whilst others are more superficial (but nonetheless helpful) differences, such as tree shape, bark colour and so on.

IDENTIFYING TREES

Identifying trees, as with any other plants, is not an easy matter, at least to begin with. A huge range of species are native to, or are cultivated within this area, and this is further complicated by the fact that horticultural varieties of many more popular species are widespread, and often rather different from their type species. However, the only way to proceed is to try it out, and one soon finds that the more trees you identify, the better you get at the whole process.

Firstly, you quickly get to recognise whole groups of species – such as willows – and can then instantly dismiss them or assign the plant you have to them accordingly. Thus you soon learn to eliminate numbers of species or families which you know your plant does not belong to. Secondly, you get to know what characters to look for in a plant, and are less easily-fooled by temporary, environmentally induced factors. This is a continuing process, and you gradually acquire more information not only about what individual species look like, but also where certain species are likely to grow, and where they do not grow, how variable they are, what they look like in winter, etc. After a while, you cease to have to look in detail at the more familiar plants, and can identify them by just their shape, colour, position, or general combination of characteristics – their 'jizz', as it is often collectively known.

What to look for

The main factors involved in identifying a tree, and used as key characteristics in this book, are tree shape and height, bark colour and characteristics, bud shape and colour, leaf shape and characteristics, flower shape, colour, scent, structure, and the characteristics of the fruit. These will be combined with non-structural information, such as flowering time, habitat, altitude, geographical area, and other factors. It is unlikely that all the information will be available at once, but you have to base your decision on as many factors as possible, of which some will be more critical than others.

The main item of equipment that you will find useful when trying to

10

Common Oak, Quercus robur, in a roadside hedge

identify trees with precision is a hand lens, of about 10x magnification. This allows details such as degree of hairiness, number of stamens, etc., to be revealed fully.

Tree shape and height Trees variably considerably in size and shape, and to some extent this is a guide to identification. Clearly, though, all trees pass through a young phase, and are therefore smaller for part of their lives.

There is also considerable overlap between most species, especially as tree height varies greatly with environmental factors. Thus, height alone is really only a useful factor when available in an extreme form; normally, you just check that your specimen, if adult, falls within the range given.

Tree shape is sometimes characteristic for a given species, but needs to be treated with caution; young, middle-aged and old specimens may have quite different shapes, as the strong dominance of the growing apex gradually subsides, giving way to more lateral growth and a general broadening of the crown. Similarly, shape varies widely according to conditions. Open-grown trees, without competition, attain their fullest extent and are often spreading, large trees; trees in an avenue, or open group will be more slender with fewer lateral branches, whilst closely-grouped plantation trees will be tall, slender, and with few side branches at all.

The direction of the wind can affect tree-shape considerably, and where there is a strong prevailing wind, trees are likely to develop strongly away from the wind direction, growing, in effect, in their own shelter. Likewise, trees at higher altitudes, exposed to frequent winds, frosts, snow-cover and other problems, will always be smaller than their lowland relatives – sometimes so small as to be ground-hugging, whilst still retaining a woody branching structure. Trees on exposed coastal headlands may show similar traits.

Finally, tree shape can be considerably affected by management. If you only ever saw Hazel growing as coppice in oak woodland, you would assume it was a multi-stemmed shrub. In fact, it is perfectly capable of growing into a small single-stemmed tree. Coppicing is the practice of cutting back a

Ancient coppiced Hazel, Corylus avellana

tree to ground level – which removes the dominance of a single apex – and allowing it to regrow as a mass of new shoots, thus producing an easily-accessible supply of fast-growing even-sized wood. Most broad-leaved trees coppice readily (though a few such as cherry do not), and some species are frequently met with as coppice. Conifers do not respond to coppicing – they normally die if cut to ground level. Other management practices include pollarding – rather like coppicing at head height or above – and hedge management, which keeps many tree species in a more juvenile, shrub-like form.

Thus tree shape and size can only be a guide, no more.

Bark coloration and characteristics are important, though rarely diagnostic. Colour may vary to some degree according to the amount of air pollution, being darker in more industrial areas, but more importantly it varies with the age of the tree; in most cases, the bark begins smoother and paler and becomes more ridged or cracked, and darker. These differences are usually noted in the text where they are useful aids to identification.

The shape and other characteristics of unopened buds may be of value in identification. Space does not allow a description of the buds of every species, but they have been described where especially significant (such as the 'sticky buds' of Horse Chestnuts), or where it helps to distinguish between otherwise similar species.

Leaf shape and characteristics are probably the most useful quick guides to identification. Whilst flowers and fruit may often hold the diagnostic characteristics, the leaves are available over a much longer period, and frequently allow instant certain identification with experience. To save repeated descriptions, leaf shapes have been given their technical terms in the text, and the important ones are shown in the diagram. The broad outline of simple leaves (a-h in the diagram) can vary with age, individual plants, and growing conditions, so these need to be assessed with care. Normally the more divided compound leaves (such as j and k in the diagram) are constant for a given species, though the number of leaflets or divisions may vary.

The texture and colour of a leaf can be helpful, though it may vary with age. Many leaves darken progressively, especially on the upper surface, as they age, so mature but not very old leaves should be looked at. Similarly, the degree of hairiness varies with age, and many leaves emerge hairy but gradually lose their hairiness. It will be noticed from the descriptions, and from examination of a variety of leaves, that the upper surface of a leaf is generally different to the lower surface. The upper surface has the function of absorbing light whilst preventing water loss from the leaf, so it is often waxy or shiny, with few hairs to impede light transfer when it is mature; the underside has the particular function of allowing gases to move into and out of the leaf through pores (stomata), whilst preventing water vapour loss if possible; thus it is often paler, with more hairs to slow down the movement of air.

Flower shape, colour, and structure can be of particular importance in assigning a tree to one family or another, though they may often be of secondary importance when identifying a tree since they may be unavailable, out of reach, or inconspicuous. If they are available, it is worth looking closely at any flowers, which should confirm or alter any preliminary identification. For example, some unrelated trees have quite similar leaves, e.g. Box Elder, *Acer negundo*, has leaves rather like an ash, *Fraxinus* species, and could be confused with it, but the flowers and fruits are quite different.

A group of flowers occurring together is known as an inflorescence, and these occur in different forms depending on the nature of the branching, the length of the flower stalks and so on. A selection of common inflorescence types is shown in opposite. In other species, the flowers may be solitary or simply grouped together in twos or threes, but in any event the character of the inflorescence is usually fairly constant for each species.

In most flowering plants, all the flowers are hermaphrodite – that is the male and female parts (stamens and carpels) are contained together in the same flower. In trees, however, it is very frequent to have separate male and female flowers. Commonly, these both occur together on the same tree, sometimes all over it, sometimes with separate areas for each. In many other cases, however, the trees are single-sex, either male or female. When looking at flowers, it is important to bear this in mind. Male flowers have several pollen-shedding stamens, usually with long filaments (stalks), whilst female flowers will have no stamens (normally), only centrally placed carpels which will develop into fruits if fertilised. Naturally, this affects whether or not you will find fruit on a given tree, whether for identification or other purposes, since only the female trees will produce fruit.

The great majority of tree flowers are wind-pollinated, perhaps making use of their greater height to catch the wind. For this reason, many tree flowers are not showy (they have no need to attract insects to them), and they often flower early, before the leaves. Insect-pollinated flowers tend to be produced later, when there are more insects around, and be more attractive. Amongst UK native trees, the limes are a good example of insect-pollinated trees, and their midsummer flowers are an irresistible lure for bees

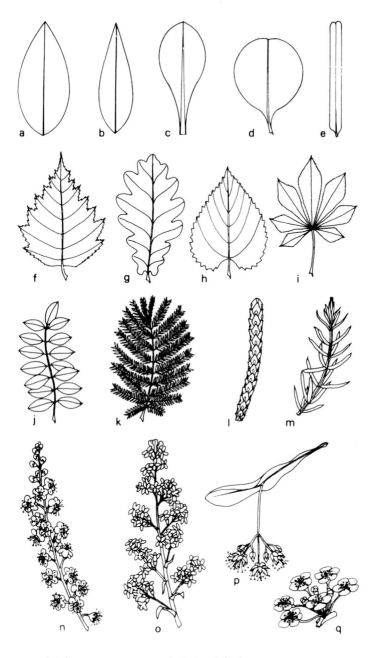

13

Leaves and inflorescences, somewhat simplified.
a ovate **b** lanceolate, tip acute **c** spathulate, tip obtuse **d** orbicular **e** linear, tip emarginate **f** tip acuminate, margin double-toothed or biserrate, base truncate **g** margin lobed, base auriculate **h** margin dentate, base cordate **i** palmate **j** pinnate, leaflets elliptic **k** twice-pinnate **l** leaves rhombic, arrangement decussate **m** arrangement whorled **n** raceme **o** panicle **p** cyme (pendent) **q** umbel

The attractive fruits of Common Spindle, Euonymus europaeus

and other insects. Most other large trees, such as beech, oak and ash, are wind-pollinated.

The characteristics of the fruit produced by trees are important factors in identifying them, or assigning them to the correct family. To some extent, it is possible to make generalisations, such as that conifers produce cones, the rose family trees (apple, pear, plum, cherry, rowan, etc.) produce fleshy, often edible, rounded fruits; and so on. In other cases, the exact characteristics of the fruit are necessary to distinguish one species from another, as in the case of various wild pear species. In other words, if fruit is available, use it to aid in identification; if collecting one to look up later, make a note of how it hung, how it was grouped, and any other information that you cannot glean from the fruit itself.

Overall, when using the book to identify an entirely unknown tree, look through the illustrations first, trying to match up as many aspects as possible between the paintings and the illustration; then check the text, which will give additional information on structural features, range and habitat, flowering time, and so on, to see if these

match, too. If so, you are probably right. If not, look elsewhere. Where there are species that could easily be confused, perhaps if only the leaves are available for example, then these are mentioned as possible alternatives.

Finally, if you begin to take more than a passing interest in tree identification, it is well worth visiting one or two tree-collections (arboreta) or botanic gardens with a good range of trees. Trees are usually well-labelled in such collections, and it gives you a chance to see a range of types in the certainty that you have the correct identification. In the UK, good examples of such places include the Westonbirt Arboretum, Glos; the Hillier Arboretum, Hants; Bedgebury pinetum, Kent, and the Royal Botanic Gardens at Kew and Edinburgh.

TREES IN THE WILD

Trees are a very dominant feature of the landscape, and we tend to take them for granted. Woods have a special place in our social history and thoughts, viewed equivocally as places of beauty, sources of products, and the direction from which danger tends to come. To understand why, we need to go back well into history.

Looking at our well-established patchwork landscapes, consisting of barely 10% woodland amongst agricultural and developed land, it is hard to imagine that things have ever been very different. Not so long ago, though, Britain – and adjacent north Europe, was wholly covered with dense woodland. When the last ice-age ended, some 10-15,000 years ago, depending on latitude and definition, Britain and the continent were still one land unit, thanks to lowered sea levels (the sea-water was all locked up in ice). As the ice sheets retreated, and the climate warmed, trees reinvaded in the wake of pioneer plants, colonising the tundra cleared by the ice. The first trees in the advance were pines, junipers and birches, followed by, and giving way to, broad-leaved trees such as elm, oak, limes, ash and others. Northern areas (e.g. much of highland Scotland) remained dominated by the hardy pioneers, especially Scots Pine, with juniper and birch, while warmer areas, including just about all of England, became dominated by broad-leaved mixed forest. Although such natural features as lightning, landslides, and grazing may have caused temporary clearings, the overall picture, in the absence of agricultural man, was one of continuous forest.

Gradually, however, man – from mesolithic times, through the Bronze and Iron Ages, Roman times and the Saxon period – began to clear woodland increasingly for hunting, then grazing animals, then arable agriculture. By Roman and Saxon times, a clear pattern of a patchwork countryside, with only a small part occupied by woodland, had emerged. This remained roughly constant through the Middle Ages, because woodland was highly valued as a source of necessary products.

By the beginning of the 20th Century, however, the pace of change quickened. Plantation forestry became much more developed, rural depopulation changed the way we looked at woodland, and greatly improved mechanical techniques in agriculture allowed the cultivation of formerly difficult land. Two world wars, with their urgent need for timber and arable land, only served to hasten the process.

Thus, the woodland we look at today is a mixture of relics of the ancient wildwood, often much altered by management, together with natural-looking woodland that has recolonised abandoned agricultural land, and plantation land, where trees have been specifically planted.

Most, but not all, trees have a tendency to form woods. They do this for several reasons. Firstly, trees are, in general, large enough to dominate other vegetation, and the appearance of the landscape. Secondly, they are very long-lived, individually, so they remain as dominant features, significant enough to be marked on maps. Thirdly, many forest trees cast a dense shade that suppresses many other species, but which does not totally prevent new trees of that species from regenerating. This makes the whole cycle self-perpetuating, at least in a stable climatic period. This gives rise to the idea of a stable 'climax' woodland, the ultimate vegetation expression for any piece of land. In practice, it is not quite as simple as this, but it is a useful idea, and it is certainly true that almost any piece of land will gradually revert to woodland if not cut, grazed or burnt, and that the tree composition of the woodland could be accurately predicted.

Woods are often spoken of as oak-woods, beechwoods, and so on, indicating the prevalence of one tree species and, indeed, many woods are dominated by one tree. Until recently, ecologists thought that this was a natural situation. It is realised now, however, that the reality is somewhat different. It has become apparent, from various studies, that most woods are naturally something of a mixture of tree species, with many of them forming part of the canopy. Over the centuries, wherever man has been active, he has selected particularly useful species, at the time, at the expense of others. Oak and beech, in particular, have been strongly favoured over ash, elm, lime and others, so that these naturally-competing species have gradually dwindled, leaving woods dominated by the commercially-valuable species, even though they may not have been planted.

However, even where woods are allowed to develop naturally, they are

15

by no means all the same. Trees, like all other plants, have particular soil, climate, and other preferences, with an optimum combination where they do best. Some trees seem to do well on almost any soil, over a wide range of climatic conditions; others do best on lime-rich soils, whilst some, such as pines and Downy Birch, prefer acid soil. Trees such as alders require a high degree of moisture in the soil, whilst Scots Pine, for example, cannot tolerate too much water. In plantations, any natural variability is smoothed out by the preparation and planting process, but in a wholly natural wood you will find endless small-scale variation with each species finding the place that suits it best.

Some trees, such as elm, tend not to form woods, while most other trees are perfectly able to grow out of woods, in hedgerows, fields or other open ground, often looking quite different when they do.

CONSERVATION AND PROTECTION OF TREES

We have seen in previous sections how great the changes in the landscape of Britain have been, as our once-dominant tree cover has gradually been eroded to produce the much more open countryside that we have now. Within historic times, the countryside has changed from being over 95% wooded to having only 5% natural woodland, which is a very considerable change. This process of change is still going on to an extent, with old woodlands still being cleared for agriculture, housing development, roads and industry. It is estimated that half of our remaining meagre stock of ancient broad-leaved woodland was cleared between 1949 and the present. Has the stage been reached when we should say that no more old woodland should be cleared?

The problem is that ancient woodland is totally irreplaceable. Old woodlands are complex, 3-dimensional

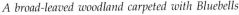

A broad-leaved woodland carpeted with Bluebells

16

structures, with many very ancient trees that have been coppiced or pollarded for generations, interconnecting networks of hundreds of species of insects, other invertebrates, fungi, flowering plants, and so on. Planted woods, even carefully-planned ones with variety and interest in mind (and most are monotonous single-species stands) do not acquire many of the species of an old wood, and little of its structure, and there is no short-cut to producing a gnarled 500-year-old oak trunk, or an 800-year-old ring of lime coppice. For this reason, old woods have to be viewed as the historic monuments, the cathedrals and churches, of the countryside. They are full of secrets, full of life, and full of interest to even the most casual walker or naturalist.

Recently, things have improved, and the rate of loss of old woods has slowed greatly. There is a growing realisation that conifer plantations, or even oak plantations, are not the same as ancient woodlands, and their historic, ecological and visual value has come to be appreciated and given more significance in decision-making.

Woods have declined dramatically in area over the centuries, as we have seen. What about individual tree species?

In general, trees have fared better than other groups of plants. Few trees have very specialised requirements, which makes them less vulnerable to change. They are also much more visible than other plants, so we notice them more readily, and it becomes obvious if they are getting rarer. No trees have become extinct in Britain in recent times, though a number have become quite rare, and others are clearly declining. Large-leaved Lime and Plymouth Pear, for instance, have both become very rare, though probably neither has been common for a very long time, if ever. Other species, such as Wild Service Tree, Black Poplar, or Juniper, have become much less common than formerly. There is little danger of any of them becoming extinct, because all can be grown readily in cultivation from seeds and cuttings, and all already exist in gardens and parks as well as in the wild. Wherever possible, though, it makes sense to conserve plants in their natural and

preferred habitat, rather than having to reintroduce them from cultivated stock, possibly of uncertain origin, once they have gone. Seed banks, botanic gardens and arboreta are all excellent back-ups, but conservation of natural habitats is undoubtedly the best way to retain our wild trees.

More recently, concern has begun to be expressed over the conservation of cultivated plants, including trees. In most cases, there is no special need to conserve an introduced tree in Britain when the tree is still common in its native country. In other situations, things are more complex. Frequently, trees which do well in gardens may be very rare in the wild, even threatened with extinction. In that case, their importance in gardens increases considerably. In a few cases, cultivated species are simply no longer known in the wild. In other examples, the plants grown in gardens are very different from the original species, by virtue of hybridisation or selection over generations. Clearly it would be a pity to lose hundreds, or even thousands, of years of horticultural development just because something goes out of fashion for a while. In such cases, official collections and arboreta play a considerable role in ensuring the survival of all our cultivated species and varieties.

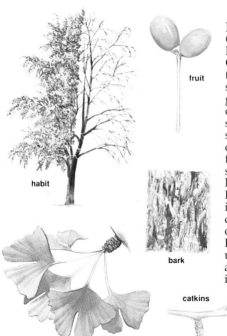

fruit

habit

bark

catkins

leaves

MAIDENHAIR TREE
Ginkgo biloba
Height: Up to 30m
Characteristics: Deciduous. Slender tree, with one or several trunks and spreading, ascending branches. Bark grey-brown, fissured and corky when older. Leaves widely spaced on older shoots, densely-packed on young shoots. Leaves distinctive, reminiscent of Maidenhair Fern in colour and form: fan-shaped, with a deep central division, yellowish to greyish-green and leathery. Petiole usually long, 1-4cm. Flowers inconspicuous; male flowers in groups of short green catkins at end of short shoots; female flowers in ones or twos at end of long pedicel, to 5cm. Fruits 2-3cm long, globose, green-grey, unpleasant-smelling when ripe. Trees are single-sex only, though flowering is sporadic, making it difficult to tell which sex they are.
Range and habitat: Chinese origin, but widely planted throughout Europe.
Similar species: None, when in leaf.

COMMON YEW
Taxus baccata
Height: To 25m
Characteristics: Evergreen. Crown broad, overall shape often almost spherical. Branches widely-spreading. Bark reddish-brown, flaking off to reveal new brighter red patches. Leaves (needles) are linear and flattened, 2-4cm long, by 3mm wide, tapering rapidly to a sharp point; unstalked, dark glossy green above, but with pale yellowish bands below. Arranged spirally on stem, but twisted to form two rows. Male and female flowers on separate trees; male flowers consist of clusters of yellowish-brown anthers in axils of leaves, shedding pollen in February; female flowers tiny, inconspicuous until the fruit begins to swell. Mature fruit is ovoid, with a hole at the tip, scarlet when ripe in autumn.
Range and habitat: A very widespread native tree, throughout the area in woods, on chalk downs, and elsewhere, but also planted widely.
Similar species: Foliage is similar to *Tsuga* and *Pseudotsuga*, though their cones are quite different.

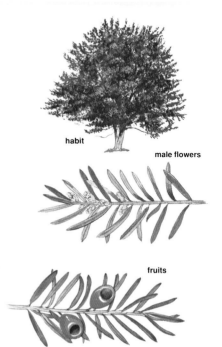

habit

male flowers

fruits

MONKEY PUZZLE
Araucaria araucana
Height: To 30m
Characteristics: Evergreen. Domed and conical in outline, though rather variable in shape. Bole usually long, narrowly-cylindrical; branches horizontal or slightly pendent, and regular. Bark grey, becoming wrinkled and scarred with age. Leaves arranged in dense spirals around shoots; individually, they are 3-4mm long, thick, dark glossy green, leathery in texture, ovate-triangular in shape. Male and female flowers separate; male cones about 10cm long, brown, in terminal clusters looking almost like dead foliage, ripe in midsummer; female cones globular, up to 15cm diameter, with golden spines, ripening and breaking up *in situ* on upper side of a shoot. Seeds brown, large (to 4cm) and edible.
Range and habitat: Native to Chile and Argentina, but very widely planted in parks and large gardens.
Similar species: Long narrow leafy branches, and shapes of cones very distinctive.

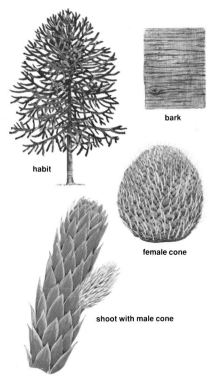

bark

habit

female cone

shoot with male cone

habit

shoot with female cone

shoot with male cones

LAWSON CYPRESS
Chamaecyparis lawsoniana
Height: Tall, to 45m high
Characteristics: Evergreen. Narrowly conical in shape, with leading shoot drooping; trunk often forked, sometimes repeatedly, bole short with branches reaching ground level in open situations. Bark greyish-brown, smooth when young but later cracking into plates. Branches numerous and small, with young shoots taking the form of flattened sprays. Leaves small and scale-like, 1-2mm, in opposite alternate pairs, closely pressed to each other; resinous parsley-like smell when crushed. Male and female flowers separate, but on same tree: male cones small (c. 4mm long) at tips of twigs, red or pink, ripening in March; female cones globose, about 8-10mm diameter, green with a bluish bloom then brown when mature.
Range and habitat: Native of western USA, but very widely planted for ornamental and commercial use in parks and gardens.
Similar species: Other *Chamaecyparis* species are similar.

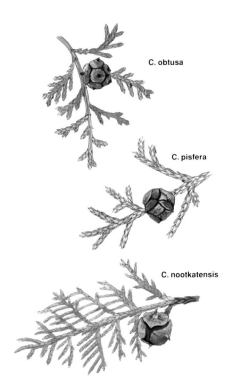

C. obtusa

C. pisfera

C. nootkatensis

HINOKI CYPRESS
Chamaecyparis obtusa
SAWARA CYPRESS
Chamaecyparis pisifera
NOOTKA CYPRESS
Chamaecyparis nootkatensis
Heights: To 30m at most, usually less
Characteristics: A group of similar evergreen cypresses, with minor differences. All evergreen. Hinoki Cypress has reddish bark, blunt green leaves, with conspicuous white markings below; Sawara Cypress has fine, incurved points to the bright green, tiny leaves; Nootka Cypress has fine-pointed leaves, with pale margins, in pendulous sprays. All share other cypress characteristics, such as the small, globular cones.
Range and habitat: Natives of Japan, or N. America (Nootka Cypress). Widely planted for ornamental use, occurring in a number of named varieties. Highly variable in stature.
Similar species: Other *Chamaecyparis* species, and the hybrid x *Cupressocyparis leylandii.*

20

LEYLAND CYPRESS
x Cupressocyparis leylandii
Height: To 35m
Characteristics: Evergreen. Arose, in various forms, as a hybrid between the Nootka Cypress and the Monterey Cypress. The bark is dark reddish-brown, with shallow vertical fissures. Branches arise regularly and ascend steeply, producing a narrowly conical tree, clothed almost to the base. Foliage and shoots generally similar to the parental genera; both male and female cones are rarely produced; male cones are c. 3mm in diameter, yellow, borne at the tips of branches; female cones are globose, 2-3cm diameter, green becoming brown, with a protrusion in the centre of each scale. The two commonest cultivars, arising from different crosses, are 'Haggerston Grey' with greyish foliage borne in several planes; and 'Leighton Green' with flattened greenish foliage branched only in one plane.
Range and habitat: Only in cultivation, where it is now very widely planted for ornament and shelter.
Similar species: Most similar to other *Chamaecyparis* species.

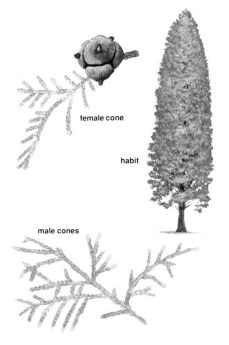

female cone

habit

male cones

MONTEREY CYPRESS OR MACROCARPA
Cupressus macrocarpa
Height: Up to 35m
Characteristics: Evergreen. Young trees are ovate-pyramidal in outline, but older trees become steadily more open and flat-topped, almost like cedars. Bark red-brown, ridged and scaly. Branches ascending in younger trees, spreading horizontally in older specimens. Foliage consists of scale-like leaves in alternate opposite pairs, with sharp darker points and pale margins; smells of lemon when crushed. Male cones carried below female cones, 3-5mm diameter, yellow, ripening in May-June; female cones are 2-4cm diameter, i.e. distinctly larger than those of *Chamaecyparis* species, green at first, becoming brown and shiny. Each scale bears a central pointed protuberance.
Range and habitat: Native to California, but very widely planted especially in southern and western areas. Common near the sea.
Similar species: None in this area is similar to mature trees.

habit

male cones

female cone

21

CEDAR OF GOA OR MEXICAN CYPRESS
Cupressus lusitanica
Height: To 30m
Characteristics: Evergreen. Generally rather similar to other cypresses, differing in a number of minor details of foliage and cones. Also, much less commonly planted, being much more frost sensitive. Bark browner, fissured into vertical peeling strips, usually on a single straight bole. Branches spreading, slightly pendent at the tips. Leaves scale-like, with spreading sharp tips, dark grey-green. Female cones smaller than those of Monterey Cypress, globular, to 1.4cm diameter, blue-grey when young, becoming brown and shiny; scales few, each with a sharp recurved boss.
Range and habitat: Native to Mexico and Guatemala, but planted through southern Europe for ornament and timber use; rare in UK in parks and large gardens in warmer less frosty areas. Various forms are found, such as var *glauca*, with bluer foliage.
Similar species: Other *Cupressus* spp.

female cone

ITALIAN CYPRESS
Cupressus sempervirens
Height: To 30m
Characteristics: Evergreen. Narrow columnar (or occasionally pyramidal) trees, that are a characteristic feature of much of southern Europe in their slender form. Bark grey-brown, ridged, often spirally. Branches are upright in common cultivated fastigiate form, but more spreading in wild form. Leaves typical cypress, small and scale-like, blunt. Male flowers ovoid, 4-6mm in diameter, yellowish-green, at tips of branchlets, shedding pollen in March; female cones more or less globose, similar to Macrocarpa but not shiny, and paler; each scale has a small point.
Range and habitat: Native to southeast Europe, but widely planted in warmer areas, mainly for ornamental reasons.
Similar species: Incense Cedar is similar in form and foliage, but the cones are quite different.

shoot with male cones

female cone

SMOOTH ARIZONA CYPRESS
Cupressus glabra
Height: To 20m
Characteristics: Evergreen. Similar to Mexican Cypress but the bark is more purplish, flaking to expose yellow or reddish-brown circular patches. Branches wide-spreading; young shoots bright orange-brown, at right angles to older shoots. Leaves scale-like, greyish-green, sometimes with a white central spot; smells of grapefruit if crushed.

Male flowers typical: abundant, yellowish, visible through winter. Female cones spherical, to 2.5cm in diameter, greenish-brown with a grey bloom, ripening dark purple-brown; scales have a small curved central spine.
Range and habitat: Native of Arizona, USA, yet hardy and widely planted in gardens and parks. Also occurs in various varietal forms.
Similar species: Other *Cupressus* species, especially Mexican Cypress.

habit

shoot with female cone

23

INCENSE CEDAR
Calocedrus decurrens
Height: To 35m
Characteristics: Evergreen. Tall thin columnar tree, rounded at the top; bark reddish-brown, divided into plates with curling edges. Bole short and narrow; branches numerous, short and ascending. Foliage like cypresses, though scale-like leaves in whorls of 4 rather than alternate opposite pairs. Male cones yellow, at tips of smaller branches, 3-4mm, producing pollen in January; female cones small, brown, ovoid and pointed, quite unlike cypress cones; the two fertile scales eventually open out. Male and female flowers on same tree.
Range and habitat: Native of western USA, widely planted for ornamental use.
Similar species: Shape is like narrower cypresses, though blunt top and different female cones distinguish it from Italian Cypress, which looks most similar in form.

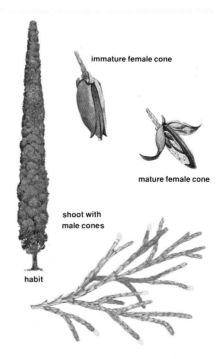

immature female cone

mature female cone

shoot with male cones

habit

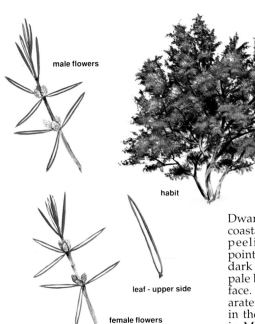

male flowers

habit

leaf - upper side

female flowers

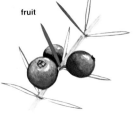

fruit

COMMON JUNIPER
Juniperus communis
Height: To 15m

24

Characteristics:
Evergreen. Conical when young, more uneven with age. Dwarf subspecies occur in mountain, coastal, and dry areas. Bark red-brown, peeling. Leaves short (to 1.5cm), pointed, stiff, in distinct whorls of 3; dark bluish-green, with a single broad pale band of stomata on the upper surface. Male and female flowers on separate trees; male flowers small, yellow, in the axils of leaves, shedding pollen in March; female cones ovoid at first, green, enlarging and darkening over 2-3 years to form the familiar 'berries'.
Range and habitat: Throughout Europe, often in extreme habitats.

PENCIL CEDAR
Juniperus virginiana
Height: To 30m occasionally, usually much less
Characteristics: Evergreen. Bark reddish brown, bole long and slender. Tree tall and slender, columnar or slightly pyramidal. Leaves are of two sorts: juvenile leaves are narrow and pointed, to 5mm, with broad pale band on upper surface, carried in pairs at ends of shoots; adult leaves, lower down shoots, are scale-like, in pairs, adpressed to stem. Foliage smells of paint when crushed. Male cones yellow, at tips of branches, shedding pollen in March; female cones plum-shaped, 4-6mm long, ripening within one year, darkening from blue-green to blue brown.
Range and habitat: Native of southern USA, planted for timber and grown for ornament as various cultivars; not in the far north.
Similar species: Similar in form to Incense Cedar and Italian Cypress, but foliage and fruit quite different. See also Chinese Juniper.

juvenile and adult leaves

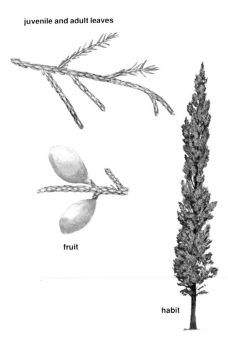

fruit

habit

CHINESE JUNIPER

Juniperus chinensis

Height: To 18m

Characteristics: Evergreen. Normally narrowly conical in shape, but variable. Bark reddish-brown, bole short. Foliage very similar to Pencil Cedar, with juvenile and adult forms; however, juvenile leaves have 2, blue-grey bands of stomata on upper surface, and are usually borne in 3s; they spread out at right angles to stems, and usually occur below adult foliage sections. Male and female flowers usually on separate trees; male flowers very small, yellow, at tips of branches, ripening in spring; female cones roughly globose, about 7mm diameter, ripening from grey to purplish-brown in their second year.

Range and habitat: Originally from China and Japan, but widely planted for ornamental reasons, in various cultivars.

Similar species: Similar to Pencil Cedar, but the foliage differs as described, and the cones are spherical not plum-shaped.

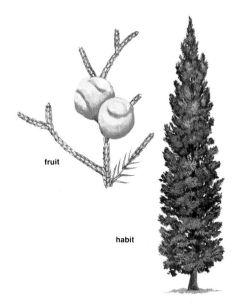

fruit

habit

25

WESTERN RED CEDAR

Thuja plicata

Height: To about 45m in cultivation

Characteristics: Evergreen. Thinly conical or triangular, with long slender bole. Bark reddish-brown, ridged and divided into plates, soft and fibrous. Leaves small and scale-like, in alternate opposite pairs, closely adpressed to the stems; glossy, dark green above, whitish below, strongly aromatic. Male and female flowers on separate trees. Male cones very small, yellowish to brownish, at tips of branches, releasing pollen in early spring; female cones roughly ovoid, 10-12mm long, with the 10 or so scales opening on ripening.

Range and habitat: Native of western USA, but widely planted for ornament and timber.

Similar species: Reasonably distinctive, especially in fruit.

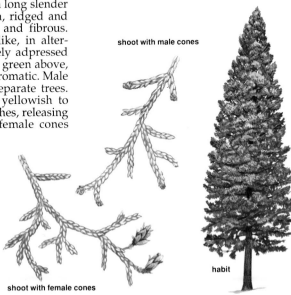

shoot with male cones

shoot with female cones

habit

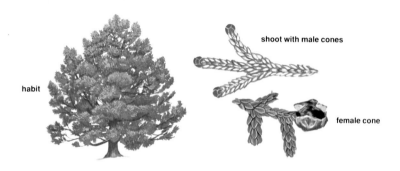

shoot with male cones

habit

female cone

HIBA
Thujopsis dolabrata
Height: To about 30m
Characteristics: Evergreen. Variable conical tree or shrub. Bark dark red-brown, dispersing at the surface into fine strips. Leaves small and scale-like, closely adpressed to stem, arranged regularly (in opposite and decussate pairs) in distinctly flattened sprays. Individual leaves are glossy green above, marked with broad white bands below, 5-7mm long, with a pointed, curved tip. Male cones small, single,

26

blackish, at the tips of branches, shedding pollen in spring; female cones solitary, roughly spherical though rather irregular, about 1.5cm diameter, becoming grey-brown when ripe. Scales, 6 to 8, with 3-5 rounded, winged seeds per scale.
Range and habitat: Native to Japan, but planted widely, mainly for ornamental reasons.
Similar species: Sometimes confused with other scale-leaved conifers, though the solitary distinctively-shaped female cones are distinctive.

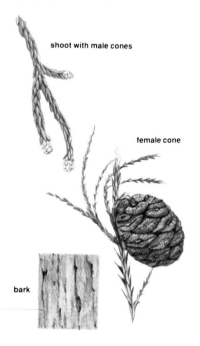

shoot with male cones

female cone

bark

GIANT REDWOOD OR WELLINGTONIA
Sequoiadendron giganteum
Height: To 100m in native USA, though rarely over 50m in N. Europe
Characteristics: Evergreen. Very large tree, narrowly conical in shape; bole markedly tapered and fluted, at base, with huge girth in older trees, bare of branches for several metres. Bark rich reddish-brown, very thick and spongy, deeply fissured. Larger holes are used by Treecreepers for roosting. Lower branches are pendulous. Foliage consisting of scale-like green leaves, up to 1cm. long, usually shorter, lacking the longer, more separate leaves of Coast Redwood. Male and female cones on same tree; male cones solitary on tips of shoots, small, yellow, ripening in spring. Female cones solitary or paired at tips of shoots, ovoid, up to 8cm long by 5cm in diameter, deep brown.
Range and habitat: Native of west coast USA, very widely planted for ornament in larger gardens and parks.
Similar species: Coast Redwood may be confused with older specimens.

COAST REDWOOD
Sequoia sempervirens
Height: To 50m in cultivation, though over 100m high in native USA habitat. Tallest tree in the world.
Characteristics: Evergreen. Tall, becoming triangular-columnar when older; trunk tapering, becoming broader, can be buttressed at base; bark reddish-brown, variable, thick and spongy, fissured and peeling. Branches horizontal or slightly pendulous. Twigs green; leaves of two types, both spirally-arranged: on leading shoots, they are appressed to stem, 6-8mm long, scale-like; side-shoots have longer leaves, to 2cm, flattened into two rows – a distinctive combination. Male and female cones on same plant: male cones terminal on main shoots, ovoid, yellow, small, shedding pollen in February-March; female cones solitary, terminal, about 2cm long, ovoid, ripening pale brown.
Range and habitat: Native of western USA, planted widely in larger gardens, parks etc., or occasionally for forestry.
Similar species: Giant Redwood, but cones and foliage distinguish it.

bark and suckers

male cones

female cone

habit

28

female cone

male cones

habit

JAPANESE RED CEDAR
Cryptomeria japonica
Height: To 50m in native east Asia, but rarely above 35m in this area
Characteristics: Evergreen. Tall, narrowly conical tree. Bole tapers rapidly at base, then gently towards apex. Bark red-brown, becoming darker, thick and fibrous, with deep vertical fissures, peeling away. Branches more or less level, in whorls. Twigs green, leaves mainly juniper-like, up to 1.5cm long, narrow pointed and distinctly curved inwards at the tips. Bright green. Male and female cones separate, on same tree. Male flowers ovoid, very small, bright orange-yellow, born in clusters of 20 or so towards the tip of branchlets, shedding pollen in February-March. Female cones ovoid-spherical, borne on larger branches, 2-3cm long, woody becoming dark brown. A distinctive feature is the groups of curved spines on each cone scale.
Range and habitat: A native of China and Japan, planted for ornament in larger gardens and parks.
Similar species: None, if cones and foliage are available.

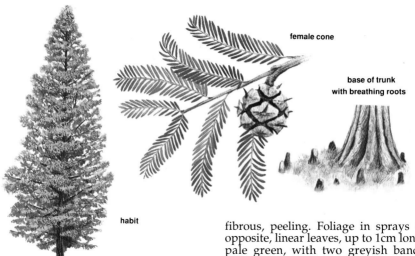

female cone

base of trunk
with breathing roots

habit

SWAMP CYPRESS
Taxodium distichum
Height: To 35-40m
Characteristics: Deciduous. Conical in shape, rather narrow. Produces distinctive knee-like roots round the trunk in wet situations. Bark pale red-brown, fibrous, peeling. Foliage in sprays of opposite, linear leaves, up to 1cm long, pale green, with two greyish bands below. Comes into leaf late, turns red-brown in autumn. Male flowers at ends of shoots, in small groups, mature in April; female cones almost spherical, 3cm diameter, green then purplish-brown; each scale has a central spine.
Range and habitat: Native of south-east USA, widely planted in parks and gardens, especially where damp.
Similar species: Dawn Redwood.

female cone

habit

male cones

DAWN REDWOOD
Metasequoia glyptostroboides
Height: To about 20m in cultivation, though taller in wild
Characteristics: Deciduous. Similar in shape to Swamp Cypress, but does not produce the root 'knees' in wet conditions. Bark paler orange-brown, flaking away in plates. Shoots greenish or purplish, slightly winged. Leaves opposite, normally distinctly larger than those of Swamp Cypress, up to 5-6cm long, pale green above, rather paler greyish below. Leaves come out earlier than Swamp Cypress, turning pinkish-red then deep red in autumn, before falling. Male cones very small, occurring in long loose clusters with each at the base of a leaf, a little back from the tip of a shoot (those of Swamp Cypress are at the tips of shoots), but rarely produced except in warmer areas. Female cones roughly spherical, about 2-2.5cm, woody, becoming brown, on long stalks; cone scales have no spines.
Range and habitat: Native to China; planted widely in warmer parts of northern Europe.
Similar species: Swamp Cypress.

shoot

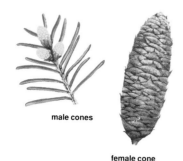

male cones

female cone

COMMON SILVER FIR
Abies alba

Height: To 55m, normally less

Characteristics: Evergreen. Tall conical to pyramidal tree, depending on age. Bole often long and free of branches. Bark dull smooth greyish-brown, becoming fissured into shallow squarish plates. Shoots hairy. Leaves spreading out into two ragged rows, several needles deep. Individual leaves variable in length, to 3cm, narrow and linear, dark green above, and with two white bands below, thick but not rigid. Male flowers ovoid, small, in groups near tips of branches, shedding pollen in March-April. Female cones produced on upper parts of higher branches of older trees, erect; roughly cylindrical in shape, tapering at each end, up to 10-15cm long, occasionally longer, green at first then orange-brown. There is a spine beneath each cone scale that becomes recurved.

Range and habitat: Native in much of central and southern Europe, as forests in mountain areas. Planted elsewhere.

Similar species: Other firs, especially *A. nordmanniana.*

30

DELAVAY'S SILVER FIR
Abies delavayi

Height: To about 25m

Characteristics: Evergreen. Generally similar to Common Silver Fir. Bark pale brown, scaly. Young twigs smooth, sometimes slightly hairy, buds resinous (unlike *Abies alba*). Leaves bright green or glossy dark green above, with margins folded down to obscure part of underside; underside with broad white bands and bright green midrib. Leaves not so clearly separated into two rows, often all round shoot. Male and female flowers separate; male flowers small, ovoid, yellowish, shedding pollen in spring; female cones produced quite frequently; erect, more barrel-shaped than those of *Abies alba*, 6-10cm high, and up to 4.5cm broad, dark purplish-green. Each cone scale has a long spine below it.

Range and habitat: Originally from China, but grown for ornament in parks and larger gardens, mainly as var *forrestii* or var *fabri*.

Similar species: Other silver firs.

shoot

female cone

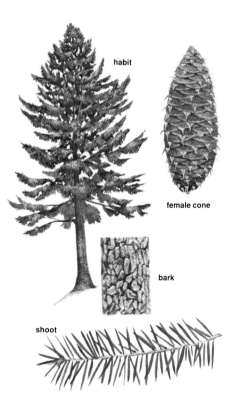

habit

female cone

bark

shoot

GRECIAN FIR
Abies cephalonica
Height: To about 35m
Characteristics: Evergreen. A tall pyramidal-conical tree. Bole tapering rapidly from ground level, then more slowly. Bark smooth grey-brown, fissuring and cracking into squarish plates. Young twigs are light brown, glabrous, buds are resinous. Leaves radiate all around the shoot, though usually with a gap below; leaves themselves are narrow, tough, to 3cm, glossy green above, with two bright white bands below; rigid, leathery, with a spine at the tip. Male flowers clustered in groups near the ends of shoots, roughly spherical, shedding pollen in spring. Female cones roughly cylindrical, to 15cm long by about 4cm wide, tapering at each end, becoming brown. Each cone scale has a triangular pointed spine, deflexed.
Range and habitat: Native to the mountains of Greece, to 1700m. Widely planted in south Europe and parts of the north, such as eastern England.
Similar species: Radiating leaves distinguish it, but Spanish Fir is similar.

31

GIANT FIR
Abies grandis
Height: To 100m in native western N. America, but more commonly to 55-60m in northern Europe

Characteristics: Evergreen. Bark smooth, dark grey-brown, cracking when older. Young twigs greenish, slightly hairy, with resinous buds. Leaves typical in shape and colour, variable in length, lying in roughly two rows in shoot. Male cones shed pollen in April. Female cones typical, erect, cylindrical, woody, ripening dark brown, up to 10cm long, 3-4cm diameter. No bracts visible on cone.
Range and habitat: Native of western N. America, planted for timber and ornamental use on larger sites.
Similar species: Most other firs similar.

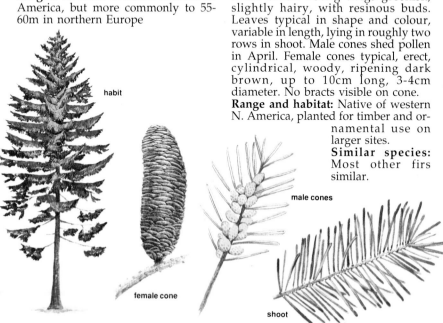

habit

female cone

male cones

shoot

ALPINE FIR
Abies lasiocarpa
Height: Up to 50m in native habitat, but generally much smaller in cultivation
Characteristics: Evergreen. Slender, tall conical-triangular tree when doing well, though usually more stunted in north Europe. Bark silvery-grey, becoming cracked. Twigs greyish-brown, foliage strongly parted into two ranks which curve forwards and upwards. Appearance of foliage is greyish because white bands below leaves are exposed by the curling. Male flowers globular, crowded on tips of shoots, releasing pollen in spring. Female cones typical of genus – erect, woody, cylindrical, up to 10cms tall by 3-4cm wide, purplish becoming brown. No cone-scale spines visible.
Range and habitat: Native of western N. America, in Cascade Mountains, occasionally planted for timber or ornament, especially in northern areas.
Similar species: Other silver firs with parted 2-rowed leaves.

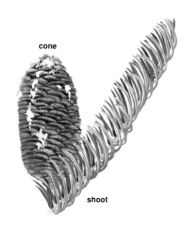

cone

shoot

32

CAUCASIAN FIR
Abies nordmanniana
Height: To about 70m in native USSR, but rarely above 45m in northern Europe in cultivation
Characteristics: Evergreen. A tall, narrow tree, sometimes almost columnar. Bole long, thin, tapering markedly at the base. Bark smooth, dull greyish-brown, eventually fissuring into plates. Young twigs greyish-brown, slightly hairy, buds not, or slightly, resinous. Leaves long and thin, to 3.5cm, glossy green above, but with white bands below; thick but still flexible, notched at tip. Separate male and female flowers. Male cones globular, in dense groups on undersides of shoots, even on lower branches, shedding pollen in April. Female cones erect, woody, cylindrical, pointed towards the top; large, up to 18cm high, 5cm wide, becoming brown; each scale has a large projecting, pointed, strongly deflexed spine below it.
Range and habitat: Native to parts of Caucasus and north-east Turkey; cultivated in northern areas.
Similar species: Other silver firs.

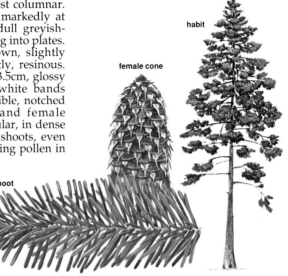

habit

female cone

shoot

habit

bark

shoot

male cones

female cone

SPANISH OR HEDGEHOG FIR
Abies pinsapo
Height: To 35m
Characteristics: Evergreen. A medium-sized pyramidal tree; bole relatively stout for size of tree. Bark smooth dark grey, becoming blacker and more fissured with age. Twigs greenish-brown, hairless, buds resinous. Leaves arranged all round stem, standing out stiffly at right angles to it; shorter than most firs (to about 2cm), sharply pointed, sometimes curved, blue-grey above, with whitish-grey bands below. Separate male and female flowers; male flowers larger than most, reddish, in groups towards the tips of branches, shedding pollen in May; female cones produced on higher parts of tree, erect, cylindrical, pale green becoming brown, to 10-15cm long, often numerous. No spines visible below each rounded cone scale.
Range and habitat: Confined as a native to mountains of south-west Spain; planted in south and central Europe for ornament, occasionally for timber.
Similar species: One of the more distinctive silver firs.

33

SIBERIAN FIR
Abies sibirica
Height: To about 30m
Characteristics: Evergreen. Trunk particularly slender, bark greyish-brown with noticeable resin blisters. Young twigs grey or fawn, with very fine pubescence. Buds resinous with grey-white resin. Leaves almost all round stems, spreading to leave a gap below. Needles thin and flexible, about 3cm long, often curved, blunt or even slightly notched at tip; colour pale yellowish-green above, with white stomatal lines below, appearing paler green than most firs from a distance. Male and female flowers separate; male flowers small, shedding pollen in spring; female cones cylindrical to egg-shaped, upright, woody, bluish at first becoming brown later, up to 8cm long.
Range and habitat: Native of north and east Russia, and extreme northeast Europe; planted for timber in other parts of northern and central Europe.
Similar species: Spanish Fir is perhaps the most similar of the firs.

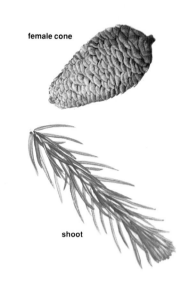

female cone

shoot

NOBLE FIR
Abies procera
Height: Up 50m
Characteristics: Evergreen. A narrowly conical tree, with a rounded top, and a stout bole. Bark smooth, grey or slightly purple, with resin blisters, becoming shallowly cracked, and darker, with age. Young twigs reddish-brown, covered by fine red pubescence, with buds resinous at tip. Leaves curving upwards strongly to leave marked gap below stem, crowded above. Individual needles 2-3.5cm long, narrow, flexible, leathery, blunt at tip, dark greyish-green, with two grey bands below. Male and female flowers separate; male flowers small, spherical, in groups on undersides of leaves, bright red, shedding pollen in May. Female cones distinctive: erect, woody, large, to 20cm high by 7-8cm wide, cylindrical, brown, with a protruding deflexed green spine below each cone scale.
Range and habitat: Native to N. America. Widely used as forest tree in northern Europe; planted throughout.
Similar species: Most firs, though cones are distinctive.

shoot

female cone

habit

34

female cone

habit

shoot with male cones

DEODAR
OR HIMALAYAN CEDAR
Cedrus deodara
Height: To 65m in native habitat, but usually 40m or less in cultivation.
Characteristics: Evergreen. Conical in outline, with a gradually pointed top. Bole short, tapering rapidly, with greyish-brown bark cracking and fissuring irregularly into small plates. Branches horizontal or slightly pendulous on mature trees, young shoots pendulous. Leaves occur in whorls of 15-20 on short lateral shoots, or spirally on branches. Individual needles 2-5cm long, with the short-shoot leaves generally shorter. They are dark green, with faint grey lines on either side. Male flowers long, 6-12cm, purplish before shedding pollen in autumn. Female cones barrel-shaped, 10-14cm high and 5-8cm diameter.
Range and habitat: Originally from the Hindu Kush and western Himalayas, but planted widely for ornamental use in larger gardens or parks, occasionally used for timber.
Similar species: Other cedars, differing mainly in shape of tree.

ATLAS OR ATLANTIC CEDAR
Cedrus atlantica
Height: To 40m
Characteristics: Evergreen. A broadly conical to pyramidal tree, becoming domed but always remaining somewhat pointed. Bark dark grey, cracking into large plates and fissuring with age. Foliage generally similar to Deodar, though young shoots are slightly ascending; often more needles in short-shoot clusters, up to 45 on a spur. Leaves 1-3cm long, shiny deep green, round in section. Male flowers generally smaller than Deodar, between 3cm and 5cm long, pinkish-yellow, shedding pollen in autumn. Female cones very similar to those of Deodar, often with hollow at top, up to 8cm high. **Range and habitat:** A native of the Atlas Mountains of Algeria and Morocco, but now very widely planted for ornamental use in parks and large gardens, occasionally for timber in warmer, drier areas. The bluish-leaved cultivar Blue Atlas Cedar, cv. Glauca, is the commonest in ornamental use. **Similar species:** Other cedars, especially Cedar of Lebanon.

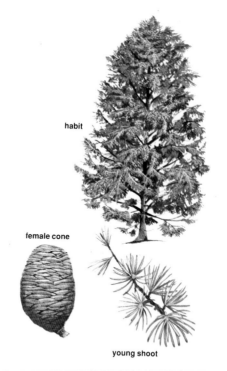

habit

female cone

young shoot

35

CEDAR OF LEBANON
Cedrus libani
Height: To 40m
Characteristics: Evergreen. Very similar in general characteristics as other cedars, especially Atlas, and they are sometimes lumped as varieties of one species. Young shoots spreading horizontally (for the tips of young shoots only, there is a useful mnemonic: Atlas-ascending; Deodar-descending; Lebanon-level). Mature trees become distinctively flat-topped and broad-domed, with large ascending main branches, level smaller branches, and separate flat plates of foliage. Foliage similar to others, though usually only 10-15 leaves in short shoot clusters. Male flowers greyish-green, 5-8cm long. Female cones as Atlas Cedar, though with rounded top rather than a hollow. The Cyprus Cedar, *C. brevifolia*, is sometimes considered as a variety of this; it has very short leaves in whorls, and is smaller. **Range and Habitat:** Native of the eastern Mediterranean, with *C. brevifolia* on Cyprus. Very widely planted ornamentally in parks and gardens; tolerant of air pollution.

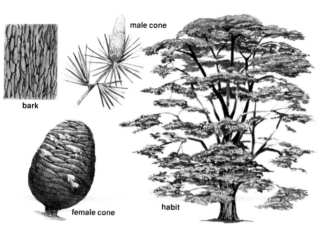

bark

male cone

female cone

habit

bark

habit

spring shoot

36

COMMON LARCH
Larix decidua
Height: To 35m, occasionally to 50m
Characteristics: Tree narrowly conical; bark rough, greyish-brown, becoming thick and fissured with age. Branches rather short, horizontal except lowest ones on old trees. Leaves in tufts containing 30-40 needles, 1.5cm-3cm long, pale green, with 2 distinct bands below. Needles turn red then yellow before falling in autumn; one of the few deciduous conifers. Female cones are soft when young in spring, with conspicuous red bracts, maturing to become woody and brown, with a blunt conical shape. Male flowers shed pollen in March-April.
Range and habitat: Native of central and east European mountains, but widely planted as a forestry and ornamental tree throughout, sometimes becoming naturalised.
Similar species: Japanese Larch, *L. kaempferi*, has female cone scales curling outwards at the tips; Hybrid Larch, *L. x eurolepis*, is a hybrid between Japanese and European larches, with intermediate characteristics.

JAPANESE LARCH
Larix kaempferi
Height: To 40m
Characteristics: Deciduous. A broadly conical tree. Generally similar in characteristics to Common Larch. Bole cylindrical, well-marked. Bark is reddish-brown and scaly. Long shoots are smooth, reddish-brown, bearing short shoots with clusters of leaves, about 40 to a cluster. Individual leaves are 2-3cm long, rather broader and more greyish than Common Larch; tree is generally leafier, with denser foliage. Male flowers borne on underside of shoots in large numbers, globular, yellowish, shedding pollen in early spring. Female cones abundant on vigourous shoots, pink or cream in spring, maturing to woody brown. Differs from European Larch in having cone scales turned outwards at tip, like individual petals of a rose.
Range and habitat: A native of Japan, but very widely planted for forestry in north-west Europe, and occasionally for ornamental use.
Similar species: Only the other larches.

spring shoot

habit

summer shoot
with cones

DUNKELD LARCH OR HYBRID LARCH

Larix x eurolepis
Height: To 35m
Characteristics: Deciduous. A vigorous tree, conical-triangular in shape. A

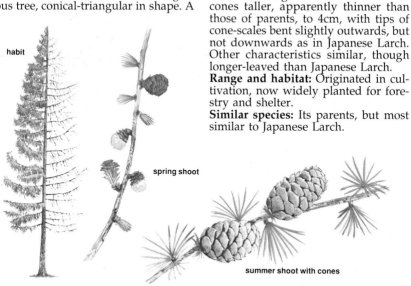

habit

spring shoot

variable hybrid between Common Larch and Japanese Larch. Typically intermediate in characteristics between the two parents, though faster-growing and often larger than either. Female cones taller, apparently thinner than those of parents, to 4cm, with tips of cone-scales bent slightly outwards, but not downwards as in Japanese Larch. Other characteristics similar, though longer-leaved than Japanese Larch.
Range and habitat: Originated in cultivation, now widely planted for forestry and shelter.
Similar species: Its parents, but most similar to Japanese Larch.

summer shoot with cones

37

DAHURIAN LARCH

Larix gmelinii
Height: to 30m
Characteristics: Deciduous. A slender, roughly conical tree, graceful. Bark reddish-brown, scaly. Branches roughly horizontal, producing large flat areas of foliage. Long shoots finely pubescent, buds resinous. Leaves roughly as other larches, in clusters of about 25, 2-4cm long, bright green above and with two, pale green-white bands below. Male flowers small and inconspicuous, shedding pollen in March-April. Female cones bright yellow in spring, becoming pinker through growing season, finally woody brown. Similar to European Larch, up to 2.5cm high, with the cone scales each having a broad, rounded tip.
Range and habitat: A native of eastern Siberia, but planted occasionally for forestry or ornament in northern areas.
Similar species: All other larches – the bright grass-green foliage is the best quick distinguishing feature.

oring shoot

habit

summer shoot
with cone

bark

habit

female cone

shoot with male cones

NORWAY SPRUCE
Picea abies
Height: To 65m in native habitat, rarely above 40m in cultivation
Characteristics: Evergreen. The familiar Christmas tree. Narrowly conical. Foliage familiar: stiff, short needles, to 2.5cm, squarish in section, spreading to expose under-surface of twigs. Individual needles borne on little pegs, as with all spruces, helping separate them from similar conifers. Female cones pendulous (unlike the erect cones of silver firs), 12-18cm long, cylindrical, bluntly-pointed, ripening brown.
Range and habitat: Native of northern Europe and mountain areas of Europe. Widely planted for Christmas trees, forestry, ocassionally for ornament.
Similar species: Other spruces.

38

habit

shoot

female cone

COLORADO SPRUCE
Picea pungens
Height: To 50m in native habitat, more commonly under 30m in cultivation
Characteristics: Evergreen. A slender conical tree. Twigs glabrous, yellowish-brown. Leaves borne all round shoot, though with more above; some curve upwards, to make foliage on upper surface much denser. Individual needles 2-3cm long, dark green in pure species, but bluish-green in most cultivars, sharply pointed, stiff. Male flowers shed pollen in May. Female cones pendent, cylindrical, long, 10-12cm, often slightly curved, purplish-brown ripening to greyer brown. Cone scales have irregularly toothed tips. The commonest cultivar is Blue Spruce, cv. Pungens, with distinctly blue foliage.
Range and habitat: Native of southwest USA, but widely planted for ornament and timber throughout most of northern Europe.
Similar species: Most spruces. The blue version of Engelmann's Spruce is most similar to cv. Pungens.

habit

cone

BREWER'S WEEPING SPRUCE OR BREWER SPRUCE
Picea breweriana

Height: To 40m high in good conditions, usually much less

Characteristics: Evergreen. A conical or triangular (when young) tree, with a long, narrow, cylindrical bole, and grey-purplish, flaking bark. Twigs pale yellow-brown or pinkish, finely pubescent. Branchlets very pendent (hence the name). Leaves spreading all around shoot, not dense, often curving outwards; individual needles narrow, distinctly flattened, 2-3cm long, sharply pointed, deep green above (paler when young), with two narrow white bands below. Male flowers large for the genus, globular, to 2cm, in loose groups. Female cones pendent, cylindrical, 6-12cm long, slightly curved, initially purplish but ripening browner. Cone scales have blunt rounded tips.

Range and habitat: Native to western USA in mountains, but now very widely planted for ornament in parks and larger gardens.

Similar species: Other spruces similar, but dark weeping foliage is distinctive.

ORIENTAL SPRUCE
Picea orientalis

Height: To 40m, occasionally more

Characteristics: Evergreen. A conical, slightly triangular tree, with dense foliage. Bole short and broad, bark pale brown with small scales. Branches slender, twigs densely hairy, whitish, pale brown with age. Leaves borne all around main stems, but more separated to expose lower surface on side shoots; very short (shorter than other spruces), less than 1cm long, glossy dark green above, squarish in cross-section, blunt. Male flowers small, ovoid, red then yellow, shedding pollen in spring. Female cones 6-8cm long, conical-slightly ovoid, often rather curved, purplish or greyish green when ripening, becoming shiny brown when mature. Cone scales broadly rounded at tips.

Range and habitat: Native to parts of Near East and Caucasus; now often planted for ornament in parks and large gardens, occasionally for forestry.

Similar species: Other spruces generally similar, but dense foliage, and very short needles are characteristic.

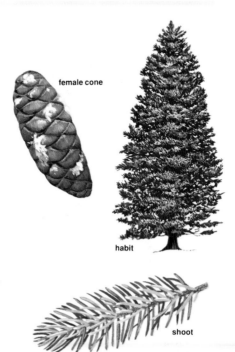

female cone

habit

shoot

WHITE SPRUCE
Picea glauca
Height: To 30m, though often smaller
Characteristics: Evergreen. A narrowly conical tree, gradually becoming broader and more round-topped with age. Bark greyish-brown or pink-brown, cracking into plates with rounded edges. Leaves borne all around shoot, but spreading more towards upper surface. Needles stand out stiffly from shoot, pointing slightly towards tip of branch. Individual needles very even in size, 1.2-1.3cm long, stiff, squarish in section, pale bluish-green, rather whiter below, distinctly aromatic when crushed, though variable in character. Male flowers shed pollen in spring. Female cones are cylindrical, slightly egg-shaped, up to 6cm long, ripening to orange-brown. Cone scales relatively few, with smoothly rounded tips.
Range and habitat: Native of Canada and north-west USA, but widely planted in northern Europe for forestry use, occasionally for ornament.
Similar species: Other spruces.
Illusrated opposite

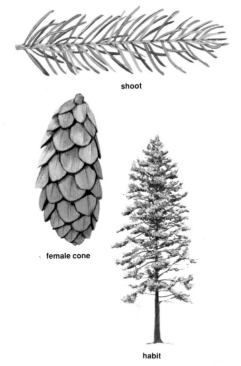

shoot

female cone

habit

ENGELMANN'S SPRUCE
Picea engelmannii
Height: To 50m high
Characteristics: Evergreen. A slender conical or rather pyramidal tree. Bole tapering rapidly from base, long and thin; bark red-brown or greyish, scaly when older. Branches ascending or curved upwards at tips. Young shoots pendulous (though not so markedly as in Brewer's Spruce). Leaves spreading to expose lower surface of twig, concealing upper surface. Needles 1.5-2.5cm long, squarish in section, flexible, pointed, green above in species, or bluish in 'Glauca' cultivar. Unpleasant smell when crushed. Male flowers shed pollen in late spring. Female cones pendulous, 4-6cm long, tapering cylindrical, slightly curved, reddish when young becoming woody brown. Cone scales squarish at tip with small teeth, purplish base to each scale.
Range and habitat: Native of west N. America, planted for forestry use in northern and central Europe, and occasionally in parks and large gardens (mainly as cultivars).
Similar species: Other spruces.

female cone

habit

shoot

SITKA SPRUCE
Picea sitchensis
Height: To 60m
Characteristics: Evergreen. A conical to triangular tree with a long spire. Bole broad, often with small shoots. Bark grey-brown, scaly, darkening with age. Leaves all round shoot but becoming parted from lower side, more crowded above. Needles flattened but distinctly keeled, 2-3cm long, sharply pointed, stiff and thick, bright green above, with two bluish-white bands below. Overall effect bluish. Male flowers shed pollen in late spring. Female cones pendent, 5-9cm, cylindrical, blunt, ripening pale brown. Scales thin and papery, with squarish, roughly toothed apex.
Range and habitat: Native to coastal N. America; often planted for timber.

mature female cone

bark

young female cones

habit

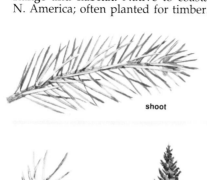

shoot

42

SERBIAN SPRUCE
Picea omorika
Height: To 30m
Characteristics: Evergreen. A narrowly conical tree, almost columnar (unusual amongst spruces). Bark orange-brown, becoming flaky. Leaves spreading away from undersurface of shoot. Individual needles 1-2cm long, flattened but keeled, blunt or short-pointed, dark bluish-green above with two whitish-grey bands below. Male flowers large, red, becoming yellow. Female cones pendent on thick, curved stalks, 4-6cm, ovoid, bluish-green ripening brown. Cone scales evenly rounded at tips, with fine teeth.
Range and habitat: Native to Yugoslavia; planted widely for timber. Tolerant of lime, acid peat, frost, pollution.
Similar species: Other spruces, though the shape of this species is distinctive.

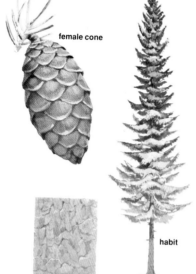

female cone

habit

bark

shoot

WESTERN HEMLOCK
Tsuga heterophylla

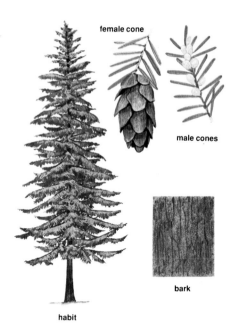

female cone

male cones

bark

habit

Height: To over 70m in native USA, but rarely above 50m in cultivation in this area
Characteristics: Evergreen. A narrowly conical or columnar tree, with dense foliage. Bark reddish-brown, becoming darker and flaking. Boles of older trees buttressed. Young shoots covered with long, pale brown hairs. Leaves parted either side into two distinct rows, made up of clearly different-sized leaves; most are either c. 0.6cm long, or 1.5-2cm long, with a blunt rounded tip, flattened, with minutely toothed margins; dark green above, with two whitish bands below. Male flowers frequent, red when young, turning yellow, shedding pollen in spring. Female cones solitary, terminal, pendent, ovoid in shape, to 2-3cm long, with relatively few blunt cone scales.
Range and habitat: A native of west N. America, widely planted for forestry, especially as a shade-bearing tree, and occasionally for ornament in larger gardens and parks.
Similar species: Eastern Hemlock.

43

EASTERN HEMLOCK
Tsuga canadensis
Height: To about 35m
Characteristics: Similar in most respects to Western Hemlock, though usually quite different in shape; trunk often forks, producing a broad squat tree. Leaves similar to Western Hemlock, though there is often a row of leaves along the mid-line of the shoot which are all twisted, exposing their white undersurfaces. Individual leaves similar, but tapering gradually from broader base to narrower tip. Male flowers similar but yellowish-green; female cones similar to those of Western Hemlock, but distinctly smaller (to 1.5cm), with cone-scale margins slightly thickened.
Range and habitat: A native of eastern N. America, but widely planted, especially in drier areas, for ornament in larger gardens and parks. Occasionally used as a forestry tree, but generally produces poor quality timber, and has no advantages.
Similar species: Western Hemlock.

habit

female cone

44

female cone

habit

bark

DOUGLAS FIR
Pseudotsuga menziesii
Height: To 100m high in native USA, often reaching over 50m in cultivation. Believed to be the tallest tree in Britain
Characteristics: A tall, slender, conical tree, with quite regular whorls of branches, supporting dense masses of pendulous foliage. Bark smooth and greyish-green, with resin blisters, but becoming more ridged and corky with age. Foliage spreading to either side of shoot; individual leaves narrow, blunt or obtusely pointed, 2-3.5cm long, grooved above, dark green on top surface, with two white bands below. Strong resinous fruity smell when crushed. Male flowers ovoid, pale, becoming yellow as pollen is shed in late spring. Female cones terminal on one-year-old shoots, pendulous, to 10cm long, ovoid in shape, ripening light brown. Bracts are distinctively 3-pointed (the tail and back legs of 'Douglas the mouse'!)
Range and habitat: Native of west N. America, widely planted for forestry, shelter, and occasionally in parks.
Similar species: Cones are distinctive.

shoot with winter bud

leaf bundles

mature cone

habit

BEACH OR SHORE PINE, LODGEPOLE PINE
Pinus contorta
Height: To 30m
Characteristics: Occurs in two distinct subspecies – var. *contorta* is the type, while var. *latifolia* is known as Lodgepole Pine. Evergreen. A small to me-dium tree with short contorted bran-ches, variable in shape. Leaves occur in pairs, 3-7mm long, variable in col-our, sharply pointed, twisted, densely packed on young shoots, more open on older shoots. Male flowers occur in dense whorls. Female cones in whorls of 2-4, pointing back down the stem, ovoid, to 6cm high, symmetrical, pale brown becoming darker. Each cone scale has a fine sharp prickle.
Range and habitat: Planted widely in Europe, particularly for forestry use in difficult areas such as reclaimed bogs.
Similar species: Other 2-needle pines, such as Corsican Pine, are similar.

45

MONTEREY PINE
Pinus radiata
Height: To 45m high, usually less
Characteristics: Evergreen. Varying in shape with age, from long pointed conical when young, becoming more high-domed when old. Bark dull grey, rugged, deeply parallel-fissured. Main branches spread wide and droop low, sometimes touching the ground. Fo-liage 3-needled, individual leaves 10-15cm long, with finely toothed margins, sharp-pointed, straight, bright green. Male flowers densely set at base of new shoots, becoming yel-low when releasing pollen in spring. Female cones occur in clusters of up to 5 around the shoot; individual cones are ovoid, usually very asymmetrical at the base, up to 15cm long (usually less), and 7-9cm at broadest point. Glossy brown, woody.
Range and habitat: Native to a limited area of California; widely planted in western areas, especially near the coast due to its tolerance of salt and expo-sure, mainly as shelterbelt.
Similar species: Combination of 3 needles and cone shape are distinctive.

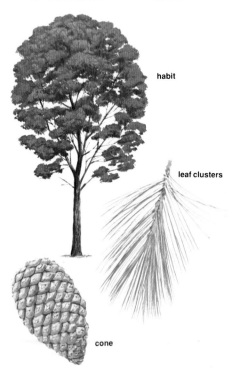

habit

leaf clusters

cone

JACK PINE
Pinus banksiana
Height: To 30m, usually much less
Characteristics: Evergreen. Variable in shape, most often raggedly conical, but becoming broad-topped with age. Bark reddish-brown, vertically fissured. Leaves in pairs, short (2-4cm long), stiff, broad, yellowish-green, twisted along their length, sharp-pointed. Foliage sparse. Male flowers numerous, yellow, shedding pollen in late spring. Female cones spherical, reddish; occur in groups of 2-3, persisting, often unopened, for years. They are cylindrical, irregularly lumpy, usually curved, pointing forwards along branch. The cone scales have no spines.
Range and habitat: Native to an area of eastern Canada around the Arctic Circle. Unusually hardy, and therefore planted widely in cold situations in mountain areas or further north. Uncommon in parks or gardens.
Similar species: Other 2-needled pines, though lumpy curved cones and short needles distinguish it.

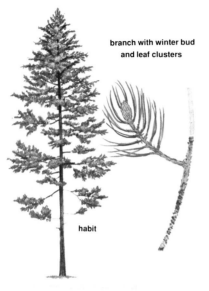

branch with winter bud
and leaf clusters

habit

cone

AUSTRIAN PINE
OR CORSICAN PINE
Pinus nigra
Height: To 50m
Characteristics: The specific name includes two subspecies often treated as different species, each with a different English name – Austrian Pine, ssp. *nigra,* and Corsican Pine, ssp. *laricio.* A large tree, triangular then flat-topped. 2-needled, with needles 10-15cm long, stiff and broad in Austrian Pine, soft and narrow in Corsican Pine. Straight or curved, dark green (paler in Corsican Pine). Male flowers shed pollen in early summer. Female cones solitary, or in small groups. Cone small, 6-8cm long, ovoid, woody, brown; cone scales have a persistent prickle on each.
Range and habitat: Austrian Pine native to mountains of central Europe; Corsican Pine from Corsica and southern Italy. Corsican Pine very widely planted for forestry, shelter and ornament, especially in difficult situations; Austrian Pine less widely-used, mainly for shelter and ornament.
Similar species: Scots Pine is probably most similar of 2-needled pines.

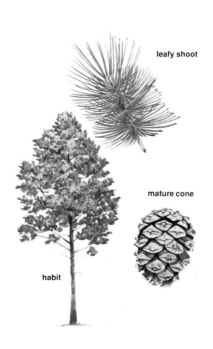

leafy shoot

mature cone

habit

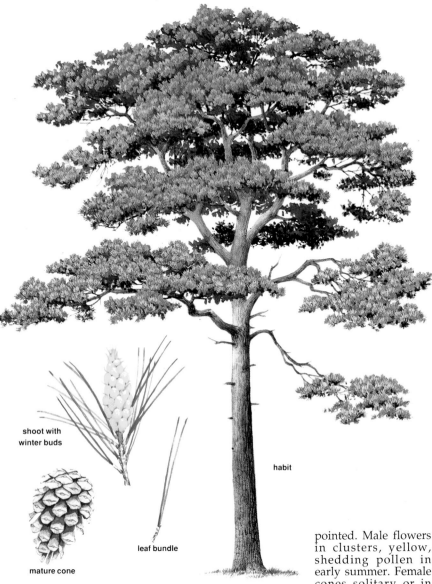

shoot with
winter buds

habit

leaf bundle

mature cone

SCOTS PINE
Pinus sylvestris
Height: To 35m, occasionally to 50m
Characteristics: Evergreen. A familiar medium-sized tree, conical at first with regular whorls of branches, but becoming distinctively open, high-crowned and flat-topped when mature. Bark reddish or greyish-brown on lower trunk, but becoming distinctively orange-red and papery higher up. Leaves in pairs, grey-green or bluish, 5-7cm long, twisted, broad, short-pointed. Male flowers in clusters, yellow, shedding pollen in early summer. Female cones solitary or in groups of 2-3, bright green and conical after a year, woody and dull brown after 2 years. Cones 5-8cm long when mature, broad-based and pointed at the top, reasonably distinctive.
Range and habitat: Native over wide areas of Europe, including Scotland, naturalised elsewhere including southern England heaths. Prefers acid soils. Also widely planted for forestry, though less now than formerly.
Similar species: Distinctive when mature.

MOUNTAIN PINE
Pinus mugo
Height: To 20m
Characteristics: Evergreen. Occurs in two forms, that have been separated into two species: *P. mugo* is the dwarf shrub-like form, *P. uncinata* is a small tree. Bark greyish-black, scaly. Leaves paired, densely set and appearing distinctly whorled, bright green, 5-8cm, curved, rather rigid. Male flowers frequent, in clusters, shedding pollen in early summer. Female cones terminal or close to ends of branches, in groups of 1-3, small (3-5cm), ovoid, becoming woody and pale brown. Cone scales have exposed part more or less flat, with a small prickle.
Range and habitat: Native of mountains of southern-central Europe, especially Alps, Pyrenees, and Balkans. Dwarfer forms are from higher altitude situations. Planted for sand-binding, and shelter through parts of northern Europe, or occasionally for forestry or ornament.
Similar species: Lodgepole Pine is probably the most similar of 2-needled pines, although detail of cone, and size of tree should separate them.

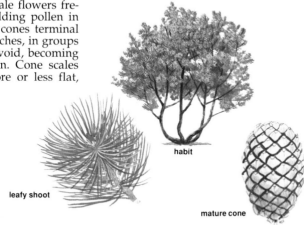

habit

leafy shoot

mature cone

48

AROLLA PINE
OR SWISS STONE PINE
Pinus cembra
Height: To 30m, occasionally more
Characteristics: Evergreen. A pyramidal or columnar tree, with thick spreading branches. Bark grey, or orange-grey, flaking off in scales on older trees. Bole short, rather thick. Twigs have a distinctive short orange-brown pubescence. Needles occur in bundles of 5, densely crowded on stem; individual needles 6-9cm long, rigid, erect, shiny dark green on outer surface, but pale bluish on inner surface, with fine white lines. Male flowers in whorls at base of short shoots, ovoid, purplish becoming yellow when shedding pollen in late spring. Female cones broad, rather squat, (to 8cm high, up to 5cm wide) purplish-red at first, ripening purplish-brown, not opening until shed.
Range and habitat: Native to Alps and Carpathians at higher altitudes. Widely planted throughout north Europe in parks and gardens, and occasionally as forestry tree for its light wood.
Similar species: None.

young shoot
with winter bud

mature cone

habit

leaves

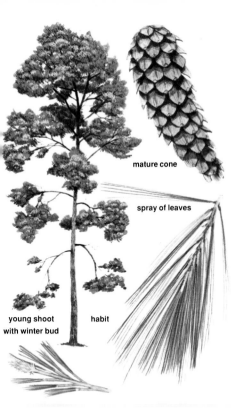

mature cone

spray of leaves

young shoot
with winter bud

habit

BHUTAN PINE
Pinus wallichiana
Height: To 50m occasionally, usually less
Characteristics: Evergreen. Tall, open, rather elegant tree when well-grown. Bark thin, grey-brown, with pinkish-brown showing in fissures, strongly ridged. Leaves in fives, held erect on young shoots, more drooping on old shoots; very long and slender (up to 20cm), greyish-green, flexible, finely toothed on margins, pointed. Male flowers spread over tree, often clustered, ovoid, yellowish, shedding pollen in early summer. Female cones long, narrow, cylindrical, up to 20-25cm long, 3-5cm broad, though opening out much wider when seeds shed. Brown, woody, becoming pendent, basal scales smaller and often reflexed.
Range and habitat: Native at moderate altitudes in the Himalayas, from Afghanistan to Bhutan. Planted widely, though rarely commonly, as ornamental in parks and large gardens, very occasionally planted for timber.
Similar species: Weymouth Pine is the most similar 5-needled pine.

cone

habit

shoot

MACEDONIAN PINE
Pinus peuce
Height: To 30m, frequently less
Characteristics: Evergreen. Conical tree, often quite narrow, with dense crown, and often branches to ground level. Bark greyish-green, smooth when young, becoming darker and more fissured with age. Leaves in clusters of five, densely set on branches, 8-12cm long, dark bluish-green in colour, narrow, flexible, finely toothed margins and a sharp point. Male flowers in clusters at bases of shoots, conical in shape, purple-tinged, becoming yellow, shedding pollen in midsummer. Female cones terminal, solitary, slender and ovoid-conical, pale green then more purplish, turning to bright green, becoming woody and brown. Mature cone 10-18cm long, narrow, pendent, often slightly curved. Cone scales have pointed, incurving tips.
Range and habitat: A native of a limited mountain area in the Balkans, but planted in a few gardens in northern Europe, and used occasionally as a mountain forestry tree.
Similar species: Weymouth Pine.

STONE OR UMBRELLA PINE
Pinus pinea
Height: To 30m
Characteristics: Evergreen. Distinctive shape, reflected in the name – mature trees are parasol-shaped, with a single trunk and radiating stout branches supporting a dense, rounded crown. Bark reddish-grey, flaking. Leaves in twos, sparse, 10-20cm long, slightly twisted, pointed, greyish-green. Cones stout, 8-15cm long, with a flat base, ripening to a light orange-brown.
Range and habitat: Native of Mediterranean area. Occasionally planted ornamentally.
Similar species: Mature trees are distinctive, by shape and cone form.

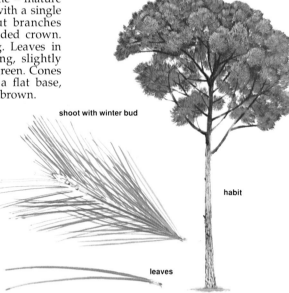

shoot with winter bud

habit

female cone

leaves

WEYMOUTH PINE
Pinus strobus
Height: Up to 50m, usually less
Characteristics: Evergreen. A largish tree, narrowly conical when young, becoming round-topped when older, with horizontal masses of foliage. Bark greyish-green and smooth at first, becoming darker and fissured with age. Young twigs more or less glabrous except for tufts of hairs below where leaf groups emerge. Leaves in fives; individual needles 8-14cm long, slender and sharply pointed, bluish-green to dark green, flexible. Male flowers small, pale, tipped with red, shedding pollen in late spring. Female cones terminal, eventually reaching 12-20cm long, cylindrical-ovoid, pendulous, often slightly curved, becoming dull brown and woody. Cone scales curve outwards on opening.
Range and habitat: Native of east N. America, planted for timber in Continental Europe, and occasionally for ornamental use.
Similar species: Distinctive, but could be confused with other 5-needled species such as Macedonian Pine.

shoot

cone

habit

BRISTLE-CONE PINE
ROCKY MOUNTAIN BRISTLE CONE PINE
Pinus aristata

Height: Rarely above 10m

Characteristics: A small, slow-growing pine, triangular in shape. In its wild state, in the Rockies, it is believed to be one of the oldest living things, exceeding 5000 years old, and growing very slowly. Leaves in groups of 5, short, rarely more than 3-4cm long, with an abrupt short point, stiff and thick. Outer surface deep green, sometimes flecked with whitish resin, paler on inner surface. Individual needles very long-lived, held close to branches densely, producing a fox-tail effect. Cones ovoid, brown, small, to 6cm long when mature. Each cone scale has a long, spreading spine in the centre.

Range and habitat: Native to a limited area of the southern Rockies into Mexico, up to high altitudes. Rare in Europe, occasionally grown in gardens or in mountain areas for timber.

Similar species: Unlikely to be confused with other 5-needle pines in this area.

BAY WILLOW
Salix pentandra

Height: To 10m, occasionally higher

Characteristics: Deciduous. A shrub or very small tree, branching low down to form a rounded bush. Bark greyish-brown, with fine cracks that show orange. Shoots shiny, olive-green, glabrous. Buds conical, pale brown. Leaves oblong-lanceolate, acuminate, wedge-shaped or sometimes rounded at base, finely saw-toothed along margins; dark glossy green above, whitish beneath, with yellow glands, leathery when mature, up to 10cm long, by 4-5cm at the broadest point. Petiole 5-10mm long, with small stipules at base that soon fall off. Catkins cylindrical, males up to 6cm long, 1cm wide, yellow when ripe; male flowers usually have 5 stamens, sometimes more; female catkins slightly smaller, curving upwards. Flowers May-June, after the leaves have opened.

Range and habitat: An uncommon native species along rivers or in marshy areas. Northern in UK, widespread in northern Europe.

Similar species: Leaf shape and size distinctive.

male catkin

leafy shoot

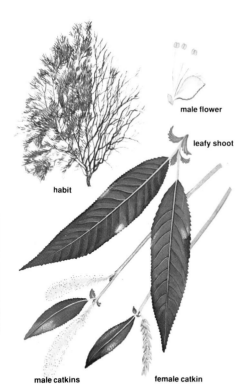

male flower

leafy shoot

habit

male catkins

female catkin

CRACK WILLOW
Salix fragilis
Height: Up to 25m high
Characteristics: Deciduous. A moderate-sized broadly conical tree, with ascending branches, but hanging leaves. Bark dark grey, scaly, becoming ridged when older.Twigs yellow-green, hairless, and 1-year old twigs snap off very easily from the base, hence the name. Leaves long, lanceolate, usually 6-9 times as long as wide, up to 15cm long, by 1.5-3.5cm wide. Shiny green above, paler bluish or greyish green below, hairless, tapering to a sharp, often curved point, coarsely toothed. Stipules present, but falling early. Petiole 1-2cm long. Catkins densely cylindrical, yellow, drooping, appearing with leaves. Male catkins shorter 2-5cm long, female catkins to 10cm, on separate trees. Flowers in April-May.
Range and habitat: A widespread and common species along rivers and ditches, through most of northern Europe except Arctic. Frequently pollarded.
Similar species: White willow is most similar, but usually has shorter leaves, with white pubescence beneath.

WHITE WILLOW
Salix alba
Height: To 25m
Characteristics: Bark dark grey, ridged, but not flaking. Young shoots pubescent, hairless later. Leaves lanceolate, acuminate at tip. 5-10cm long by 1cm broad, finely-toothed, with long, white hairs closely pressed to leaf surface. Dark green above, white below. Stipules fall early, petiole 5mm long. Catkins long, cylindrical. Male catkins 7-8cm long, abundant, yellow-green; female catkins shorter, green.
Range and habitat: Very common in wet places, throughout.
Similar species: Crack Willow, Weeping Willow.

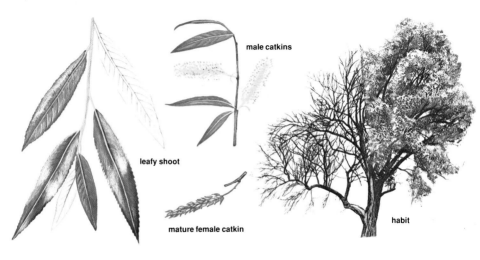

male catkins

leafy shoot

mature female catkin

habit

WEEPING WILLOW
Salix x chrysocoma
Height: To 25m
Characteristics: A hybrid between White Willow and Chinese Weeping Willow (*S. babylonica*), producing a tree with weeping habit and silky leaves. Broadly similar to White Willow, with long narrow leaves covered with silky hairs above and below, making them appear white. Catkins similar to those of White Willow; most trees are male only. The most distinctive feature of the hybrid is its weeping habit; it produces several large branches low down, which curve outwards; smaller branches are level, whilst younger shoots hang straight down like curtains – the familiar 'Weeping Willow' form.
Range and habitat: Widely planted for ornamental use in parks and gardens, especially in wet situations.

leafy shoot

habit

male catkins

ALMOND WILLOW
Salix triandra
Height: To 10m
Characteristics: A shrub or, occasionally, a small tree, spreading out into a broad roughly triangular bush. Bark is smooth, grey-brown, flaking off patchily. Shoots hairless, except when young, red-brown in colour. Leaves variable, ovate or oblong-lanceolate, 3 to 7 times as long as wide, acutely pointed, rounded at the base, symmetrical overall. They are hairless, dark rather glossy green above (less so than Bay Willow), paler grey-green below. Petiole 0.5-1.5cm long, with large persistent toothed stipules at the base. Catkins cylindrical, erect, appearing at the same time as the leaves in March-May; male catkins slender, greenish-yellow, to 5cm with 3 stamens; female catkins shorter.
Range and habitat: Widespread and fairly common in wet places, throughout north Europe, except the high Arctic. Rare in Wales, and almost absent in Scotland.
Similar species: Bay Willow is most similar.

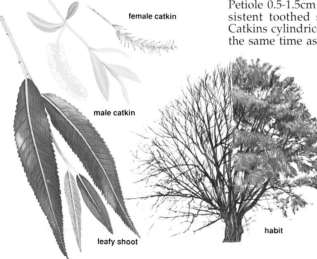

female catkin

male catkin

leafy shoot

habit

habit

leafy shoot

female catkin

male catkin

male flower

SALIX BOREALIS
Height: To 10m
Characteristics: A shrub or small tree, with ascending irregular branches, producing a triangular-rounded bush. Young shoots densely pubescent. Leaves are ovate or oblong, 4-7cm long, between 2 and 4 times as long as broad, acute or shortly acuminate, with evenly, fine-toothed edges, and a rounded or wedge-shaped base. They are leathery, dark green above, paler greyish beneath with a mass of long whitish hairs, becoming greener in mature leaves. Catkins cylindrical-ovoid, appearing with the leaves in May-June, on thick densely woolly stalks. Both sexes yellowish-green, female catkins appearing white when in fruit. Male catkins to 2.5cm long, short-stalked; female catkins to 3cm long in flower, much longer when in fruit (to 8cm).
Range and habitat: A species of wetlands and tundra in the far north of Europe, not occurring in Britain.
Similar species: None in area.

54

SALIX PEDICELLATA
Height: To 10m, usually less
Characteristics: A shrub or small tree, with grey bark. Young shoots greyish, downy, becoming smooth with age. If bark is peeled off, wood shows promi-

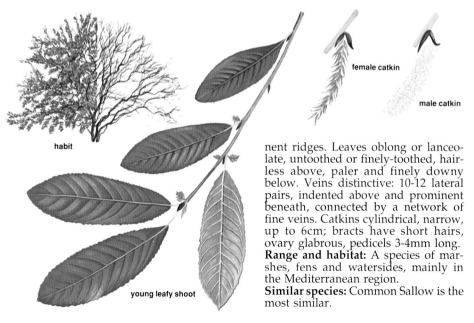

habit

female catkin

male catkin

young leafy shoot

nent ridges. Leaves oblong or lanceolate, untoothed or finely-toothed, hairless above, paler and finely downy below. Veins distinctive: 10-12 lateral pairs, indented above and prominent beneath, connected by a network of fine veins. Catkins cylindrical, narrow, up to 6cm; bracts have short hairs, ovary glabrous, pedicels 3-4mm long.
Range and habitat: A species of marshes, fens and watersides, mainly in the Mediterranean region.
Similar species: Common Sallow is the most similar.

EARED SALLOW
Salix aurita
Height: To 2.5m
Characteristics: A small shrub, with numerous spreading branches; twigs slender, pubescent at first but becoming glabrous, brown, angular and branching at a wide angle, with raised striations under the bark. Leaves oval to oblong, wedge-shaped at base, markedly wrinkled, dark green above, paler and downy below, with a distinct point that is often curved; stipules are large and conspicuous (the 'ears' of the name), toothed, and persistent. Catkins cylindrical to oval, up to 2.5cm long, appearing before the leaves in April-May, persisting, with black-tipped green scales.
Range and habitat: Widespread in damp places, by water and on moors throughout much of Europe except the far north and south.
Similar species: Distinctive by the broad, wrinkled leaves, and large stipules.

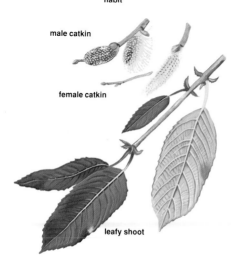

habit

male catkin

female catkin

leafy shoot

COMMON SALLOW
Salix atrocinerea
Height: To 10m, occasionally higher
Characteristics: Most commonly a rounded spreading bush, but may occasionally grow out into a conical tree, especially in woodland. The nomenclature of this group is somewhat confused; 'Common Sallow' refers both to *S. atrocinerea* and *S. cinerea*, and *S. atrocinerea* is now generally viewed as a subspecies of *S. cinerea*. Twigs downy grey-brown, with raised stripes on the wood, visible if the bark is peeled off. Leaves oval, green above, glaucous below with rusty hairs, toothed, to 4cm long; petiole 1cm long, with small narrow stipules. Catkins familiar as one of the 'pussy willows' (male catkins), ovoid, 2-3cm long, yellow stamens, appearing before leaves; female catkins longer. Both appear in March-April.
Range and habitat: Common throughout Britain and northern Europe, except the far north, in wet places, and by rivers and still water.
Similar species: Goat Willow is similar, but larger in all parts, without the stripes on the wood.

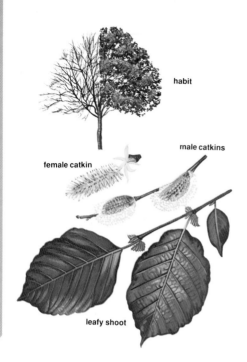

habit

male catkins

female catkin

leafy shoot

GOAT WILLOW, GREAT SALLOW OR PUSSY WILLOW
Salix caprea

Height: To 10m high, usually less

Characteristics: Deciduous. Separate male and female plants (like most willows). Commonly a rounded shrub with a short twisted trunk, occasionally a small tree. Generally similar to Common Sallow, though larger in most respects. Leaves larger, 6-12cm long, broader and more rounded, margins entire or shallowly toothed; wood under the bark of 2-year-old twigs not raised into striations. Stipules large, much broader than those of sallow, petiole about 1cm. Catkins appear before the leaves in March-April, occasionally earlier; male catkins familiar, ovoid, with yellow stamens, 2-3.5cm long; female catkins cylindrical, becoming 5-7cm long eventually, pale green with blackish-tipped bracts.

Range and habitat: Wet places, damp scrub, woodlands, by streams etc. throughout most of northern Europe except the far north. Very common.

Similar species: Common Sallow.

56

leafy shoot

female catkin

SALIX XEROPHILA
Height: Up to 6m, occasionally more
Characteristics: A rounded shrub, or occasionally a small tree, with erect branches. Shoots dull and woolly, buds strongly angled, conical, reddish-brown in colour. Leaves oblong, about 3cm long, with untoothed margins, woolly grey with long appressed curving hairs, paler below than above. Lateral veins well-marked, in 7-8 pairs from strongly-defined midrib. Petiole 3-7mm, stipules usually absent. Catkins lax, appearing before the leaves in April-June, 1.5-3cm long, on long (2-3cm) stalks.
Range and habitat: Not in UK. A northern European species, mainly Scandinavian, in tundra and waterside habitats.
Similar species: *S. starkeana* is very similar, but dwarfer, with stipules present, and less woolly leaves, occurring in similar habitats and area, as far south as Germany. Almond Willow could be confused, but leaves are larger and shinier.

COMMON OSIER
Salix viminalis
Height: To 3-5m, occasionally to 10m
Characteristics: A shrub or small tree, but frequently pollarded in cultivation to produce whips for basket-making. Leaves very long, from 10-25cm, narrow, 1-2cm; usually at least 6-12 times as long as broad. Base narrow and wedge-shaped, upper surface green, undersurface whitish with hairs, margin wavy, untoothed, often curled under.

Stipules small and narrow, falling early. Male catkins appear before the leaves; females appear with the leaves, with black-tipped bracts.
Range and habitat: Native through lowlands of Britain, and throughout central Europe. Occurs in wet places.
Similar species: Hoary Willow.

female catkins

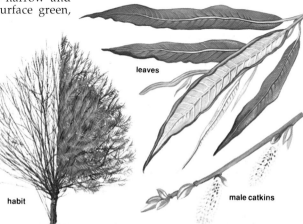

leaves

habit

male catkins

HOARY WILLOW
Salix elaeagnos
Height: To 6m, occasionally to 15m
Characteristics: A triangular-ovate shrub or small tree. Similar to the Common Osier. Leaves long and narrow, but tend to taper continuously from the base to the apex, up to 12cm long, by about 1cm wide. Both surfaces woolly when young, but upper surface becoming almost hairless brighter green, underside greyish. Margin often curled over, very finely toothed. Petiole c. 0.5cm, stipules absent. Catkins longer and thinner than those of Osier, appearing with the leaves.
Range and habitat: Not in UK. Common in parts of northern Europe, from France north-eastwards, in wet places, not in Scandinavia.
Similar species: Common Osier.

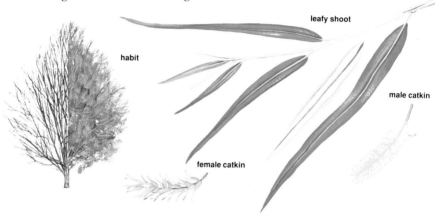

leafy shoot

habit

male catkin

female catkin

58

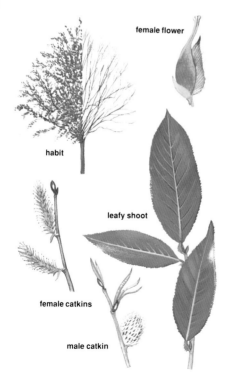

female flower

habit

leafy shoot

female catkins

male catkin

VIOLET WILLOW
Salix daphnoides
Height: To 10m
Characteristics: A rounded-triangular large shrub or small tree. Shoots distinctively dark shiny purple, especially in var. *acutifolia*, covered with a waxy bloom. Buds blackish-purple. Leaves ovate-lanceolate, 2-4 times as long as broad, to 10cm long, dark green and shiny above (when fully developed), greyish-white below. Margins finely toothed, petiole short (to 4mm), stipules large and heart-shaped. Catkins ovate-cylindrical, 3-5cm long, about 1.5cm broad, appearing before the leaves, in March-April. Male catkins yellow, female catkins narrower and greener; both have blackish-tipped bracts.
Range and habitat: Not in UK. Common in Scandinavia in wet habitats, on tundra, and by rivers. Widely cultivated in gardens, especially as var. *acutifolia*, for its purple stems in winter.
Similar species: Purple Willow, *S. purpurea*, has purplish stems when young, less marked, otherwise Violet Willow is distinctive.

WHITE POPLAR
Populus alba
Height: To 30m
Characteristics: Bark of young trees and branches is smooth and grey-white, but darker and rougher on older parts. Leaves vary: those on long shoots are 3-5 lobed, up to 12cm long, dark greyish-green above, downy white beneath; leaves on short shoots smaller, narrower, greyish below. Male and female trees separate; male catkins pendent, grey, 4-7cm long, with red stamens; female catkins becoming longer, green. Flowers March-April.
Range and habitat: Widely planted, especially near coasts.
Similar species: Grey Poplar.

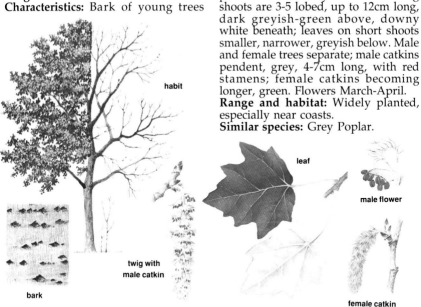

habit

leaf

male flower

twig with male catkin

bark

female catkin

59

GREY POPLAR
Populus x canescens
Height: To 40m
Characteristics: A large tree with a broad crown; suckers readily around the base. Bark grey and smooth at first, becoming more fissured and darker with age. Branches few, large, ascending, with younger twigs descending. Leaves similar to White Poplar, but less deeply divided or palmate, with more rounded or blunt, large teeth, dark green above, greyish below; leaves of the short shoots are ovate or almost circular. Catkins similar in appearance and timing, catkin scales more deeply cut than in White Poplar.
Range and habitat: Widespread through north-west Europe as riverside native, but also planted.

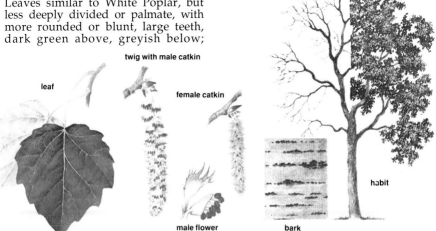

twig with male catkin

leaf

female catkin

male flower

bark

habit

habit

60

bark

mature leaf

leaf from sucker

male catkins

ASPEN
Populus tremula
Height: To 20m, usually less
Characteristics: A variable tree, most often narrowly conical, though becoming broader when mature; usually a short-lived pioneer tree. When mature, bole often leans slightly, and produces abundant suckers. Leaves distinctive and attractive, almost round with uneven sinuous rounded teeth all around the margin; usually 5-6cm across, occasionally larger, thin and soft, bright green above, paler below. Petioles long, 4-6cm, flattened. Leaves tremble even in light breeze, showing pale undersurface, and making a distinctive rustling. Male and female flowers on separate trees; male catkins pendulous, to 4cm long, with numerous white hairs; female catkins similar, but slenderer and elongating to 10-12cm when fruit ripens. Produced in March, before the leaves.
Range and habitat: A common and widespread species throughout except in the far north, in woods, on heaths and damp ground.
Similar species: Distinctive.

BALSAM POPLAR
Populus balsamifera
Height: To 25-30m high
Characteristics: Deciduous. A medium-sized tree, narrowly conical, eventually producing a broad crown, suckering freely from the base. Bark thin and shallowly fissured, grey-brown. Branches erect or steeply ascending; young shoots and buds thickly covered with resin, appearing varnished. Leaves roughly ovate, with a long point, 5-8cm long, finely toothed on the margins, dark shiny green above when mature (but red when emerging, then pale green at first), paler below, rather downy. Petiole long, 2-5cm. Leaves on suckers often larger – tree leaves are more useful for identification. Male catkins 7-8cm long, rather pendulous, greenish; female catkins longer; both produced in April-May, just as the leaves are opening.
Range and habitat: A common N. American species frequently planted for forestry use etc., especially in wet sites such as river valleys.
Similar species: Western Balsam Poplar.

leaf

habit

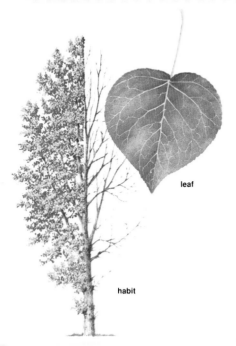

leaf

habit

WESTERN BALSAM POPLAR
Populus trichocarpa
Height: To 35m
Characteristics: Generally similar to, and closely related to, Balsam Poplar; hybrids between the two occur, and they are a confused group nomenclaturally. Forms a medium-sized narrowly conical tree, sometimes broadening later. Differs from Balsam Poplar in not producing suckers around the base, often producing small epicormic branchlets on the lower trunk instead. Bark grey-brown, becoming fissured with age. Leaf similar in colour to that of Balsam Poplar, but shorter and rounder, with a heart-shaped base (more wedge-shaped in Balsam Poplar), and a shorter point. Catkins and flowering period as for Balsam Poplar.
Range and habitat: A native of west N. America, widely planted in northern Europe especially in river valleys and wet places, rarely naturalised. Hybrids with Balsam Poplar also planted.
Similar species: Balsam Poplar. Black Poplar has similar leaf shape, but not sticky buds.

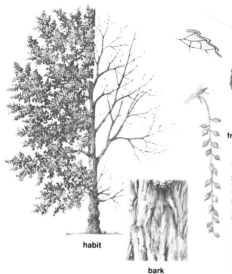

habit

bark

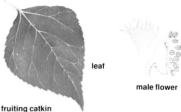

leaf

male flower

fruiting catkin

BLACK POPLAR
AND LOMBARDY POPLAR
Populus nigra, incl. cv. italica
Height: To 30m
Characteristics: Deciduous. A distinctively-shaped tree, with an uneven, rounded crown, a massive short bole that becomes covered with bosses, and spreading, arching branches; often leans distinctly. Leaves ovate-deltoid, sharp-pointed, with small teeth, dark green above, paler green below (but reddish-green when young). Petiole flattened, 3-4cm long. Male catkins cylindrical, pendent, narrow, to 5cm long, becoming crimson. Female catkins greenish, pendent, to 7cm long in flower, much longer in fruit. Flowers in March-April as leaves emerge.
Range and habitat: Native to parts of central and western Europe. Occurs sparingly, usually as single trees, by ponds, roadsides, etc. Lombardy Poplar has narrow, columnar shape, and is widely planted.

Lombardy Poplar

HYBRID BLACK POPLARS
Populus x *canadensis*
Height: To 45m, usually less
Characteristics: The name refers to a complex of hybrids that have arisen at different times between the N. American Cottonwood, *P. deltoides*, and the European Black Poplar. A number of types have specific varietal names, of which the best known is 'Serotina' the Black Italian Poplar, and these names are probably more useful than the hybrid name. Although variable, the hybrids are intermediate between the parents, lacking the trunk bosses of Black Poplar, whilst retaining the ciliate leaf margins of Cottonwood. The Italian Black Poplar, 'Serotina', has red-brown leaves in spring, becoming pale green later.
Range and habitat: Black Italian Poplar is very widely planted as a screen, windbreak, and ornamental tree over much of Europe; var. *regenerata* is particularly common in France. The hybrids do not naturalise.
Similar species: Both parents are similar.

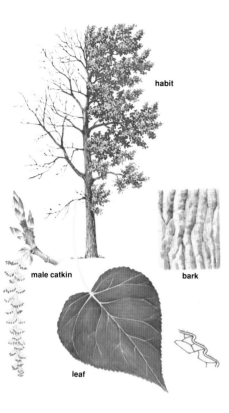

habit

male catkin

bark

leaf

COTTONWOOD
Populus deltoides
Height: To 30m, sometimes more
Characteristics: Deciduous. A broadly conical tree, with a broad crown, and robust bole, free of bosses and epicormic growths. Very fast-growing. Branches ascending, without the marked downward curve found in older Black Poplar branches. The young twigs have distinct angles and the buds are sticky. Leaves longer than wide, triangular with a long point, with a heart shaped base (cf. wedge-shaped in Black Poplar, roughly straight in the hybrids), and a long petiole. The leaf margins are ciliate (i.e. covered in short, erect, even hairs). Female catkins become very long when mature (up to 20cm).
Range and habitat: Originally from eastern N. America, but widely planted for timber, and along roadsides, throughout central Europe, but not Scandinavia. Naturalises occasionally, in damp warm places.
Similar species: Hybrid Black Poplars are most similar; the leaf shape is the most useful quick guide.

63

SHAGBARK HICKORY
Carya alba (= *C. ovata*)
Height: To 30m

Characteristics: Deciduous. Separate male and female flowers on same tree. Ovate-conical in shape, developing a broad crown; bark distinctly shaggy, grey, peeling in long scales (hence the common name). Leaves pinnate, with, usually, 2 opposite pairs of leaves and one large terminal leaflet, up to 20cm long. Leaf margins sharply toothed, with tufts of whitish hairs between each tooth. Fruit roughly spherical, 4-6cm diameter, green.
Range and habitat: Native of N. America. Planted for timber, and occasionally for ornament, especially in south-west Britain.
Similar species: Walnuts, superficially.

habit

flowers

leaves

male catkins

wintering twig

fruit

CAUCASIAN WINGNUT TREE
Pterocarya fraxinifolia
Height: To 35m
Characteristics: Deciduous. A moderate-sized tree with a broad spreading crown. Trunk often splits into several main branches low down. Leaves large,(up to 60cm long), alternate, with pinnate leaflets in 10-20 pairs, and one terminal leaflet. Leaflets 10-15cm, broadly lanceolate, toothed, with a midrib with long hairs below. Main leaf stem is rounded, with a swollen base, yellowish-green. Female catkins pendent, cylindrical, long (15cm in flower, but 2-3 times as long in fruit). Fruits distinctive, hanging down in long groups, with each fruit having a circular whitish-green wing surrounding it.
Range and habitat: Native of SW Asia, including the Caucasus. Planted widely but sparingly, mainly in large gardens.
Similar species: Walnuts have similar characteristics, but the winged fruits are distinctive.

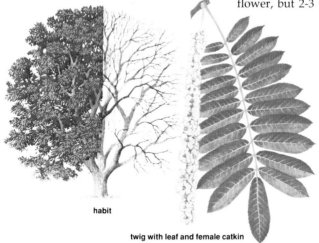

habit

twig with leaf and female catkin

64

leafy twig with fruits

BLACK WALNUT
Juglans nigra
Height: To 30m, occasionally to 50m
Characteristics: Deciduous. A tall domed tree, with a well-developed bole. Bark dark brown or blackish, with a diamond-like pattern of fissures and ridges. Broadly similar to Common Walnut, though readily identifiable on close examination. Leaves pinnate, with 6-12 pairs of leaflets (most commonly 7), and one terminal leaflet, total length to 45cm. Leaflets lanceolate, pointed, toothed, 6-12cm long. Male flowers similar to those of walnut; female flowers in fives, with greyish-green hairs (cf. green in Common Walnut), fruit solitary or in pairs, green, globose, smooth. Flowers in May-June.
Range and habitat: A N. American species, planted in central Europe as a timber tree occasionally, and in gardens for ornament.
Similar species: Common Walnut, and Caucasian Wingnut. The Butter-nut, *J. cinerea*, (not described) is similar, with longer hairy fruits.

habit

COMMON WALNUT
Juglans regia

Height: To 30m

Characteristics: Deciduous. A broad, wide-spreading tree with a rounded crown. Bark grey, smooth though becoming fissured. Main branches several, large, curving, small branches numerous. Buds dark purple-brown. Leaves alternate, pinnate, up to 45cm long, with 3-4 pairs of leaflets and one terminal one; individual leaflets rounded, elliptical or obovate, 8-15cm long, mostly untoothed, short-stalked, thick and leathery. Male catkins long, reaching 12-15cm, cylindrical, yellowish, appearing in April-May before leaves, or just as they open. Female flowers terminal, greenish, in clusters of 2-5. Fruit familiar, globose to slightly egg-shaped, green, 4-5cm diameter, shiny, smooth.

Range and habitat: Native to southeast Europe and much of Asia, but very widely planted through Europe, except far north, for ornament and its nuts. Naturalises in warmer areas.

Similar species: Black Walnut and Caucasian Wingnut.

leafy twig with fruits

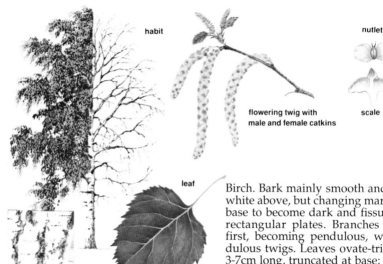

habit

nutlet

flowering twig with
male and female catkins

scale

leaf

bark

SILVER BIRCH
Betula pendula
Height: To 30m
Characteristics: Deciduous. A familiar tree, but often confused with Downy

Birch. Bark mainly smooth and silvery white above, but changing markedly at base to become dark and fissured into rectangular plates. Branches erect at first, becoming pendulous, with pendulous twigs. Leaves ovate-triangular, 3-7cm long, truncated at base; margins with uneven teeth, with a series of large teeth separated by smaller ones. Male catkins long, yellow, in small groups; female catkins in leaf axils.
Range and habitat: Widespread, particularly on light soils, throughout. A colonising species, short-lived, and intolerant of shade. Also widely planted.
Similar species: Other birches.

DOWNY BIRCH
Betula pubescens
Height: To 25m
Characteristics: Generally similar to Silver Birch. A small tree. Bark smooth, greyish or brown, not as silvery as Silver Birch, but not markedly different at the base; may be fissured, but not broken up into rectangular bosses. Branches and twigs not strongly pendulous; young branches finely pubescent. Leaves similar to Silver Birch, but more rounded, with even teeth,

white hairs in vein axils below, and with a hairy petiole. Catkins similar to Silver Birch. Flowers in April-May.
Range and habitat: Similar range to Silver Birch, though often on more acid soils or harsher environments, where it may form woods. Less often planted.
Similar species: Other birches.

leafy twig with fruiting catkins

bark

nutlet

scale

habit

PAPER-BARK BIRCH OR CANOE BIRCH
Betula papyrifera
Height: To 30m in native US habitat, but rarely exceeding 20m in N. Europe
Characteristics: Deciduous. Unmistakably a birch. A medium-sized conical tree, with strong ascending branches. Bole robust and well-marked; bark distinctively smooth and silvery-white, peeling off in papery strips (hence the name). Often has patches of pinkish or pale orange on bark. Shoots warty. Leaves broadly similar to other birches: 5-10cm long, pointed, dark green, not shiny, thick and rather leathery; paler below, with tufts of hairs in a few leaf axils. Petiole robust and hairy. Leaf margin double-toothed. Male catkins larger and longer than other two species, up to 10cm long, cylindrical, yellow-green.
Range and habitat: Native to northern N. America, but grown widely (though uncommonly) as a specimen ornamental tree in parks and larger gardens.
Similar species: Other birches, though bark is very different from the two native species.

67

GREEN ALDER
Alnus viridis
Height: To 6m
Characteristics: Deciduous. A shrub, most commonly branching close to the base to form a rounded bush, with erect branches. Buds shiny and reddish-brown. Leaves 4-6cm long, ovate or almost circular, but pointed, sharply double-toothed around the margin, and hairy on the veins below; petiole grooved. Catkins appear with leaves in spring. Male catkins pendulous, up to 10cm long, yellow when ripe. Female flowers small, green, becoming ovoid brown cones in groups of 3-5.
Range and habitat: A central European mountain species.
Similar species: Other alders.

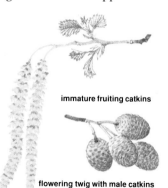

immature fruiting catkins

flowering twig with male catkins

leafy twig with female catkins

habit

scale

nutlet

COMMON ALDER
Alnus glutinosa
Height: To 25m, usually less
Characteristics: Deciduous. A small-medium tree. Bark grey-brown. Leaves roughly circular, blunt or slightly notched at apex, 5-10cm long, wavy-edged or shallowly-toothed; dark green, shiny. Catkins appear before leaves, in March-April: male catkins in clusters of 2-3, purplish-brown, pendulous, to 4cm; female catkins reddish when young, short, ovoid, stalked; ripening into clusters of 3 or so woody brown cones.
Range and habitat: Common in wet places in Britain and most of Europe; occasionally planted for ornament.

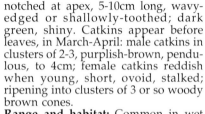

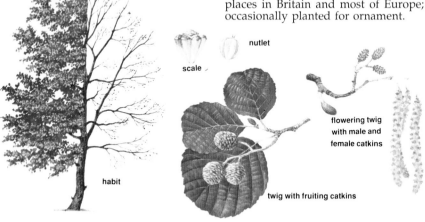

nutlet

scale

habit

flowering twig with male and female catkins

twig with fruiting catkins

68

GREY ALDER
Alnus incana
Height: To 25m
Characteristics: Generally very similar to, and often confused with, Common Alder. Differs in several respects. Shoots are covered in downy grey pubescence when young, disappearing later. Leaves ovate, or occasionally round, more sharply toothed, dull green above and greyer below; pubescent all over when young, usually on veins only when mature. Female flowers on very short, pubescent stalks.
Range and habitat: Native to mountain regions of central Europe, often in drier habitats than Common Alder, but now widely planted throughout as tree for difficult situations, such as reclamation sites. Also in gardens, occasionally.
Similar species: Italian Alder, *A. cordata*, is generally similar, with more dense foliage, pointed dark green leaves that have large tufts of orange hairs in vein axils below, grey bark, and male catkins in groups of 3.

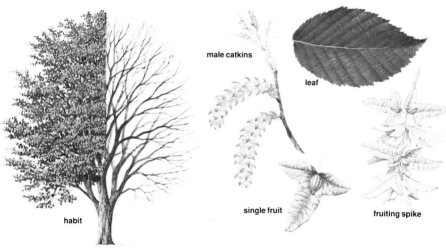

male catkins

leaf

habit

single fruit

fruiting spike

HORNBEAM
Carpinus betulus
Height: To 30m, usually less
Characteristics: Deciduous. A medium-sized, rounded tree, with a twisted, fluted bole in older trees; often pollarded. Bark silvery-brown, becoming fissured with darker areas. Leaves ovate, sharply pointed, 5-10cm long, with sharp double teeth, dark green above, paler below. Male catkins, pendulous, to 5cm, greenish-yellow with some red scales; flowers April-May. Fruiting clusters of 6-8 pairs of nuts, each with a large green 3-lobed bract.
Range and habitat: Native to most of Europe in woods and hedgerows; sometimes planted.
Similar species: Unmistakable in fruit.

69

cluster of nuts

leaf

HAZEL
Corylus avellana
Height: To 12m, usually less
Characteristics: Deciduous. Frequently coppiced to produce small dense multi-stemmed bushes. Shade-tolerant. Familiar for its male catkins in spring, and nuts in autumn. Leaves almost round, raggedly double-toothed, heart-shaped at base, with petiole hairy. Male catkins appear before leaves, January-March, with inconspicuous female flowers, with bright red styles. Nuts well-known, with 1-4 nuts surrounded by green bracts.

habit

twig with male and female flowers

Range and habitat: Very frequent throughout most of Europe, as understorey in woods and in hedges.
Similar species: Similar hazel species occur in southern Europe.

habit

70

bark

leaf from mature tree

nuts

spring shoot with flowers

BEECH
Fagus sylvatica
Height: To 40m
Characteristics: Deciduous. A large, graceful, high-domed rounded tree. Bark grey, smooth, sometimes becoming rougher. Large branches ascending or arching gracefully. Buds long and thin with tapering point, red-brown. Leaves ovate, pointed, 5-10cm, with wavy untoothed margin; opening pale green, fringed with white silky hairs, becoming darker and less hairy later. Male flowers in rounded clusters on a long stalk, yellowish-green; female flowers usually paired, small, developing into familiar 'beech nuts' with 4-lobed prickly involucre containing the brown shiny mast. Flowers in April-May, beechmast ripens in October.
Range and habitat: Widespread through most of central and western Europe, forming woods frequently, on drier lighter soils, and extensively on mountain slopes. Also planted for timber and ornament in parks and gardens, often in varietal form.
Similar species: Southern Beeches, *Nothofagus* spp., have similarities.

RAOUL, RAULI
OR SOUTHERN BEECH
Nothofagus procera
Height: To 30m
Characteristics: Deciduous. A largish broadly conical tree, with a slender bole, horizontal branches at base, and ascending branches higher up. Bark greenish-grey, becoming evenly fissured later. Buds thinly conical, noticeably angled, about 1cm long, bright reddish-brown. Leaves roughly ovate, rounded or wedge-shaped at base, shortly-pointed; margin wavy and finely toothed, underside with silky hairs on veins; the most obvious characteristic is the deep furrowing where the 14-20 pairs of side veins lie. Male flowers solitary, in leaf axils, appearing in May; female flowers in groups, producing 2-3 fruit in a 4-lobed, heavily fringed cup, in autumn.
Range and habitat: Native to southern S. America, used as a forest tree locally for its rapid growth, and planted for ornament in larger gardens.
Similar species: Roble Beech, possibly Common Beech.

nuts

habit

71

ROBLE BEECH
Nothofagus obliqua
Height: To 30m, occasionally more
Characteristics: Deciduous. Generally similar to Raoul, and often confused with it. Differs in that: Bark greyish, becoming cracked and fissured into squarish plates, with curling-up edges, in older trees (the cracks are mainly vertical in Raoul). The twigs have a markedly regular herring-bone branching pattern, spreading downwards from the branches. Buds smaller, to 5mm. Leaves roughly ovate, with irregular ragged toothed margins, sometimes lobed. There are 6-11 pairs of veins, which are impressed, but not so deeply furrowed as in Raoul leaves. Nuts smaller, to about 6mm.
Range and habitat: A native of Chile and Argentina, widely planted for timber due to its exceptionally fast growth rate (over 1.5m per year recorded); also planted for ornament in parks and large gardens throughout northern Europe.
Similar species: Raoul is most similar, though Roble Beech could be confused with Common Beech at a casual look.

habit

72

bark

fruit

SWEET CHESTNUT OR SPANISH CHESTNUT
Castanea sativa

Height: To 35m

Characteristics: Deciduous. A familiar tree through much of Europe, both as a standard tree and coppiced. Bark brownish-grey, becoming vertically furrowed and often spiralled. Leaves long oblong-lanceolate, 10-25cm, dark glossy green above, paler below, with marked regular spiny teeth along the margins. Petiole about 2cm long. Flowers usually in long bisexual greenish-yellow catkins, with a few female flowers at the base, then a long cylinder of male flowers, reaching 30cm long at most. Flowers in May-July. Fruit familiar, in groups of 2-3, comprising green very spiny outer coating, splitting into 4 to show 3 brown shiny chestnuts. Often small in north.

Range and habitat: Native to W. Asia and possibly southern Europe, but very widely planted and naturalised on acid or light soils, throughout northern Europe except the far north.

Similar species: Distinctive in flower or fruit.

leafy twig with flower spike

leaf

RED OAK
Quercus rubra
Height: To 35m
Characteristics: Deciduous. A large, broadly conical tree. Bark silvery-grey or brownish-grey, smooth, sometimes becoming fissured. Leaves 10-20cm long, strongly lobed, with the deepest ones dividing the leaf about halfway to the middle. Each lobe has several bristle-tipped teeth on it. Leaves dark matt green, greyer below. In autumn, they turn rich red before falling. Petiole 2-3cm, with a strongly swollen, reddish base. Acorns ovoid, flattened at base, 2cm long, in shallow evenly-patterned cup, which is finely downy, on stout 1cm long stalk.
Range and habitat: Native of N. America, but widely planted for timber in central Europe, and for ornament in parks and gardens throughout.
Similar species: Leaf shape distinguishes it from most other oaks.

bark

habit

acorn

73

KERMES OAK
Quercus coccifera
Height: To 5m
Characteristics: Evergreen. A shrub or small tree, usually occurring as a rounded untidy bush. Bark dull grey, smooth or finely patterned in older trees. Main branches are numerous, often arising near the base, ascending and dividing repeatedly to form a shapeless bush. Twigs yellowish at first, covered with branched hairs, becoming smoother later. Leaves hollyleaf shape, 2-4cm long, spiny, leathery, rather stiff, dark green above and almost as dark green below (not markedly paler, as in Holm Oak). Petiole short. Acorns small, 1.5cm, ovate, with a shallow cup thickly covered with stiff spiny scales; the acorns ripen in their second year, remaining on the plant for very long periods. Originally the host plant for coccid insects, cultivated to produce red dye (hence the scientific name).
Range and habitat: Warmer areas of southern-central Europe, not in UK.
Similar species: Holm Oak, Cork Oak.

habit

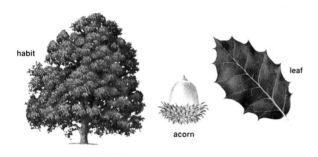
leaf

acorn

HOLM OAK
Quercus ilex
Height: To 30m
Characteristics: Evergreen. A broadly-domed rounded tree, often branching low down. Bark brownish-black, cracked into shallow rather square plates. Twigs grey-brown, downy. Leaves oblong to ovate or sometimes lanceolate, 6-10cm long, pointed at tip, rounded at base; margin normally wavy but untoothed on older branches, but often spiny-toothed on young trees, similar to Kermes Oak. Blades thick, dark green above, pale greyish below with raised veins. Petiole 1-2cm long, densely hairy. Male flowers very conspicuous April-May as sprays of pendulous golden catkins; acorns ovate, pale green, 1.5-2cm, almost half enclosed by cup which is covered by rows of small downy scales.
Range and habitat: Native to south Europe, but very widely planted throughout except in far north, often naturalising, especially near coast.
Similar species: Cork Oak and Kermes Oak are most similar.

habit

leaf

bark

acorn

74

habit

leaf

bark

acorn

CORK OAK
Quercus suber
Height: To 20m
Characteristics: Evergreen. A medium-sized rounded tree, with several large twisted branches from quite low down. Most distinctive feature is the bark - pale greyish brown, divided up into thick ridges and furrows, becoming distinctly winged if left to grow, extremely corky. Leaves holly-like, ovate with well-spaced spiny teeth on a wavy margin, (occasionally untoothed) up to 7cm long; dark green and smooth above, pale grey-green and pubescent below. Petiole about 1cm long, densely pubescent. Acorn ovoid, 2-3cm long, with cup covering about half; scales on cup long and projecting outwards. Flowers in May-June. The bark is the source of commercial cork, harvested in south Europe, leaving trees orange-trunked.
Range and habitat: Native to south-west Europe, where it is widely planted. Planted for ornament in UK and central Europe, not common.
Similar species: Holm Oak, though the bark is very different.

TURKEY OAK

Quercus cerris

Height: To 40m

Characteristics: Deciduous. Conical tree, becoming more broadly domed with age. Branches ascending, often swollen at base. Bark grey-brown, fissured, eventually forming squarish plates. Leaves 10-12cm, roughly oblong but regularly lobed with a series of 6-10 pairs of lobes or large teeth, indented roughly halfway to the midrib; upper surface dark green, rather rough, lower surface greyish, pubescent at first; petiole 1-2cm, pubescent. Leaves on cut shoots or hedges may be very variable. Acorns ovate, roughly half enclosed in cup which is covered in long pointed scales, curving outwards. Flowers May-June, acorns ripen in October.

Range and habitat: Native to southern Europe, but widely planted further north both for timber and ornamental use. Naturalises readily.

Similar species: Common Oak most similar, though leaf shape and acorn cups are quite different.

habit

leaf

acorn

acorn

habit

leaf

SESSILE OAK OR DURMAST OAK

Quercus petraea

Height: To 40m

Characteristics: Deciduous. Roundly domed in shape, from a distinctly straighter, often longer, bole than Durmast Oak. Branches radiating around trunk, also straight. Bark grey-brown, fissured vertically. Buds orange-brown with long white hairs. Leaves obovate, wedge-shaped at base (or slightly heart-shaped), strongly and rather regularly lobed with 6-8 pairs of rounded lobes; flat, dark green above, paler below, with long hairs along veins; no reflexed auricles at base of leaf (see Durmast Oak), petiole 1-2.5cm. Acorns long ovate, in groups with no stalk or very short one. Male catkins pendulous, green, in May.

Range and habitat: Very widespread native tree, often forming woods, commonest on lighter more acid soils; in Britain, mainly an upland species now. Not often cultivated.

Similar species: Common Oak is most similar. Hybrids occur.

HUNGARIAN OAK
Quercus frainetto
Height: To 30m
Characteristics: Deciduous. Bark grey, finely and deeply fissured. Buds grey-brown, surrounded by persistent scales. Leaves oblong, 15-25cm long, narrowing to wedge-shaped base; margin deeply lobed with 4-8 pairs of blunt, forward-facing lobes, which are broadly toothed; green above, greyer below. especially when young. Acorn short and rounded, cup occupying about 1/3rd of the length, with small pubescent closely-adpressed scales.
Range and habitat: Native to south-east Europe; planted sparingly in parks and large gardens.
Similar species: Common and Sessile Oaks, though leaf shape is different.

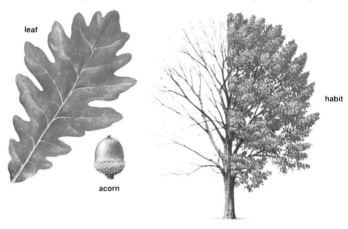

leaf

acorn

habit

76

habit

acorn

leaf

DOWNY OAK
Quercus pubescens
Height: To 25m
Characteristics: Deciduous. Smaller than most oaks, forming a medium-sized tree or large shrub. Bark is dark grey, (darker than Sessile or Common Oak),finely and deeply fissured into small rough plates. Main branches swollen where they join the trunk. Twigs and buds densely pubescent. Leaves broadly similar in shape to those of sessile oak, usually narrower and more parallel-sided; greyish-green and hairless above, but densely grey-pubescent when young, gradually becoming less so, leaving just clusters of hairs along midribs by autumn. Petiole pubescent. Acorns long-ovoid, similar to Sessile Oak, with pubescent cup-scales, on short stalks.
Range and habitat: Native of southern Europe as far north as north France, where it forms woods extensively, but planted elsewhere sparingly for ornamental use.
Similar species: Similar to Sessile Oak, with darker bark, more hairy parts, and generally different habitat.

habit

acorn

bark

leaf

COMMON OAK, ENGLISH OAK OR PEDUNCULATE OAK
Quercus robur
Height: To 40m
Characteristics: Deciduous. A very familiar tree. Large, broadly and irregularly domed, with large low twist-ing spreading branches. Similar in general characteristics to Sessile Oak, and often confused with it. Differs in having a less straight, less clearly-defined bole, less straight branches, and more clustered foliage. Buds pubescent later becoming hairless. Leaves roughly similar, but more irregularly lobed, tapered towards base which usually has a pair of distinct curled auricles; petiole shorter, less than 1cm. The upper surface is dark green, lower surface paler, pubescent when young becoming hairless later. Acorns carried in groups of about 3 on a long stalk, 4-8cm long.
Range and habitat: A very common and widespread species in Britain and much of Europe, especially on heavier soils, in woods and in the open.
Similar species: Sessile Oak.

WYCH ELM
Ulmus glabra

Height: To 40m

Characteristics: Deciduous. A large, broad tree. Bark smooth and grey when young, more cracked and ridged with age, and turning browner. Young twigs dark red-brown with short stiff erect hairs. Leaves 10-18cm long, ovate, abruptly acuminate, with base usually distinctly uneven, with longer side overlapping the short, hairy petiole. Margin roughly and sharply toothed; upper surface dark green, with short stiff hairs, paler below. Flowers in early spring before the leaves; male and female parts in same flower. Occur as reddish, unstalked clusters, dominated by red-tipped anthers; fruits produced soon after, often before leaves open, as clusters of bright green, circular-oval membranes with seed in centre, becoming papery brown. Various hybrids between Wych Elm and *Ulmus minor* occur, collectively known as Dutch Elms. They have slightly narrower leaves than pure Wych Elm, with a distinctly longer stalk (1-2cm), and smoother, shinier upper leaf surfaces.

Range and habitat: Common and widespread, especially in north and west Britain, and most of Europe. Dutch Elms are commonly planted.

Similar species: Other elms.

leafy twig

flowering twig

fruit

habit

78

ENGLISH ELM
Ulmus procera

Height: To 35m

Characteristics: Deciduous. A tree with a very distinctive outline: a long trunk persisting towards the crown, few large ascending main branches, numerous small branches but nothing in-between; suckers freely. Leaves quite small, to 10cm, rounded to ovate, base rounded and unequal, but larger side not overlapping petiole: upper side of leaf rough. Fruit rare.

Range and habitat: Once common in England and some parts of Europe, but devastated by Dutch Elm disease.

Similar species: Other elms – leaf detail and tree shape are important recognition features.

fruit

bark

leafy shoot

habit

Fruits of Wych Elm

THE *ULMUS MINOR* GROUP OF ELMS

Height: To 30m

Characteristics: A rather confusing roup of elms, easily distinguished from Wych Elm and English Elm, but difficult to separate amongst themselves. The group includes Smooth Elm, Plots's Elm, Coritanian Elm, and Cornish Elm, though both English and scientific names are rather confused. *U. minor* is a medium-sized, conical tree, often suckering, with deeply-ridged, grey-brown bark. Winter buds are shiny, ovoid, dark red and slightly downy. Leaves 6-10cm long, roughly ovate, tapering to a long point, shiny dark green above, paler below with tufts of hairs in the vein axils; there are 7-12 pairs of leaf veins. Flowers typical of elm, fruits ovoid, with an off-centre seed close to the notch in the wing margin. Within the group, the following may be distinguished: Smooth Elm, *U. carpinifolia*, has leaves widest above the middle, with a straight midrib; Coritanian Elm, *U. coritania*, has leaves widest at or below the middle, with midrib curving towards the shorter side and leaf base very unequal; Cornish Elm, *U. angustifolia*, is a narrowly conical tree, with leaves broadest above the middle, midrib straight, and base roughly equal; Plot's Elm, *U. plotii*, is a narrow tree, with an arching leading shoot; leaves narrow, midrib straight, base symmetrical. *U. canescens* is similar to this group, but has downy twigs and leaves.

Range and habitat: Smooth Elm is widespread throughout much of Europe both as a native and as a planted species. Coritanian Elm occurs in south-east Britain, Cornish Elm in south-west Britain, Plot's Elm is more widespread, and *U. canescens* is a Mediterranean species.

80

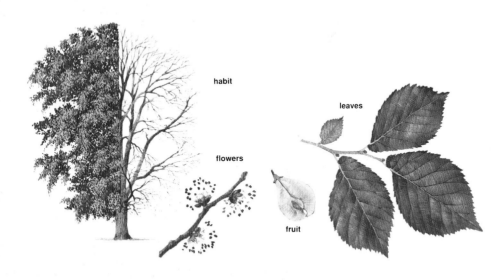

habit

leaves

flowers

fruit

EUROPEAN WHITE ELM OR FLUTTERY ELM
Ulmus laevis
Height: to 35m
Characteristics: A large tree, rounded and wide-spreading, with an untidy broad crown. Bark grey or brown, smooth when young, but becoming deeply ridged later. Twigs reddish-brown, rather hairy. Leaves round or oval, 7-12cm long, with a short tapering point, and double teeth all around the margin. The asymmetrical base is very pronounced in this species, with one side of the leaf beginning much higher up the petiole than the other; there are 12-19 pairs of veins, with 2-3 more on the longer side. Upper surface of leaf smooth or finely pubescent; lower surface grey with down. Flowers borne in clusters in early spring, on very long pedicels, 4-6 times as long as the flowers.
Range and habitat: Not native in UK, but widespread in central and eastern Europe; occasionally planted for shelter and ornament, rarely in UK.
Similar species: Similar to other elms, but long-stalked flowers, and markedly uneven leaves are distinctive.

1-year twig with flowers

fruit

habit

82

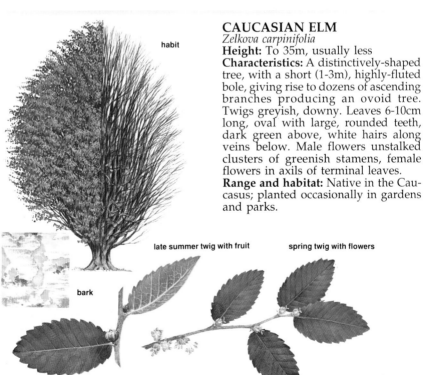

habit

CAUCASIAN ELM
Zelkova carpinifolia
Height: To 35m, usually less
Characteristics: A distinctively-shaped tree, with a short (1-3m), highly-fluted bole, giving rise to dozens of ascending branches producing an ovoid tree. Twigs greyish, downy. Leaves 6-10cm long, oval with large, rounded teeth, dark green above, white hairs along veins below. Male flowers unstalked clusters of greenish stamens, female flowers in axils of terminal leaves.
Range and habitat: Native in the Caucasus; planted occasionally in gardens and parks.

late summer twig with fruit

spring twig with flowers

bark

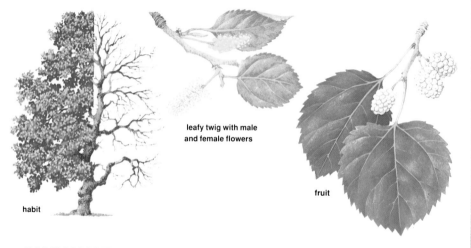

leafy twig with male
and female flowers

fruit

habit

COMMON MULBERRY OR BLACK MULBERRY
Morus nigra
Height: To 12m
Characteristics: The familiar fruit-bearing mulberry. A broad, rugged uneven spreading tree, with a short rough bole, and twisted branches. Bark dark orange, fissured and burred. Leaves ovate-triangular, with a heart-shaped base, toothed margins, sometimes lobed; deep shiny green above, paler below. Petiole stout, to 2.5cm. Flowers in cylindrical spikes, pale greenish, in separate male and female groups, produced in May. Fruit ripens to deep red then very dark before falling; edible.
Range and habitat: Native to Asia, but cultivated in southern Europe. Frequently planted in parks and gardens.
Similar species: White Mulberry.

83

WHITE MULBERRY
Morus alba
Height: To 16m
Characteristics: Similar to Common Mulberry in foliage and form, and occasionally confused with it, though much less common. Leaves similar to those of Common Mulberry, but very variable, though usually with a smooth upper surface (rougher in Common Mulberry). The main difference lies in the flowers and fruits; both male and female flowers occur in longer cylindrical spikes, with longer pedicels (to 2cm). Fruit similarly-shaped, but white, pink or purplish, not deep red-black. Edible, but not especially good. The favoured foodplant of silkworms.
Range and habitat: Chinese in origin, but widely cultivated historically; found occasionally in gardens and parks of northern Europe.

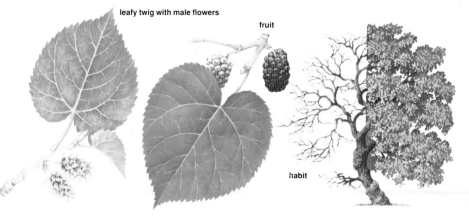

leafy twig with male flowers

fruit

habit

fruiting shoot

FIG
Ficus carica

Height: To 6m, often much less

Characteristics: Deciduous. A low spreading shrub or small tree, often with a distinct slender bole, topped by wide-spreading branches. Away from southern Europe, most frequently grown as a dense shrub against walls. Bark smooth grey, with darker markings. Leaves borne alternately, palmately-lobed (with 3-5 lobes), up to 20cm long or broad, on a long petiole; leathery in texture, dark green above, paler below with very prominent veins – the 'fig leaf' of literature. The flowers are produced, unseen, on the inner surface of an inverted pear-shaped receptacle that is almost closed at the top, with pollination taking place through this hole. This develops into the familiar sweet, edible fig in its second year.

Range and habitat: Probably originally native to south-west Asia, but long-cultivated in southern Europe. Planted for ornament, and occasionally fruit, in parks and gardens of northern Europe.

Similar species: None.

habit

flowering shoot

CHILEAN FIREBUSH
Embothrium coccineum
Height: To 12m
Characteristics: Evergreen. A shrub or small tree, with dark purplish bark, and sinuous ascending branches from a short bole. New shoots pale green, smooth, rather pendulous. Leaves unlobed and untoothed, variable in shape though usually roughly ovate. Deep bluish-green above, paler below. Peti-ole about 1cm long, bright green. Flowers distinctive, occurring in clusters of terminal, or axillary, bright red tubular flowers, which separate into 4 parts at the apex revealing a long yellow-orange stigma; total length about 5-10cm long. Flowers in May and June.
Range and habitat: A S. American species (Chile-Argentina) widely planted in gardens and parks.
Similar species: None.

85

KATSURA TREE
Cercidiphyllum japonicum
Height: To 20m, occasionally more
Characteristics: Deciduous. An ovoid-conical medium-sized tree, with a single or multiple trunk, and grey-brown bark, which eventually becomes fissured. Shoots slender, with conspicuous opposite pairs of glossy brown buds. Leaves in opposite pairs, ovate or nearly round, up to 8cm long,short-pointed at tip, cordate at base, with shallow rounded teeth; blue-grey above, greyer below, but emerging pinkish and turning red in autumn; petiole 2-4cm long. Male and female flowers borne on separate trees: male flowers are tufts of red stamens borne in the nodes before the leaves emerge; female flowers are clusters of dark red styles. Fruit occur in green claw-like clusters.
Range and habitat: Of Japanese origin, now widely planted in gardens and landscaping schemes.
Similar species: Foliage very similar to Judas Tree, but that has pea-like pink flowers borne on the wood, and alternate leaves.

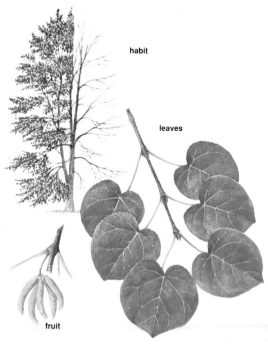

habit

leaves

fruit

TULIP TREE
Liriodendron tulipifera
Height: To 40m tall
Characteristics: Deciduous. A large tree, with a single trunk, becoming wide-spreading, with large lower branches, when old. Bark greyish, evenly-ridged, becoming more orange when old. Leaves characteristic, squarish with 4 lobes, a broad flat notched apex, 10-18cm long, shiny green above, paler and waxy below: petiole long, to 10cm. Flowers hermaphrodite, large, cup-shaped, more like Magnolias than Tulips, predominantly yellowish-green.
Range and habitat: A southern USA species, widely planted in parks and large gardens.

flowering shoot

habit

EVERGREEN MAGNOLIA OR BULL BAY
Magnolia grandiflora
Height: To 15m
Characteristics: Evergreen. A medium-sized broadly conical tree, with large spreading branches, sometimes from the base. Bark smooth, dark grey. Leaves elliptical-oblong, to 15cm long, hard, leathery and thick, untoothed though often wavy-edged, glossy above, matt below with rust-coloured pubescence. Flowers large (to 25cm diameter), solitary, creamy-white, fragrant, borne sparsely but over a long season (July-November).
Range and habitat: Native to south-eastern USA; widely planted as a park and garden tree, often against walls.
Similar species: Other Magnolias, but this is the only evergreen, glossy-leaved species.

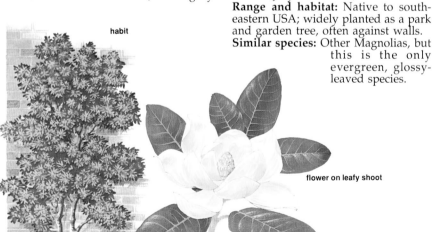

habit

flower on leafy shoot

SWEET BAY
OR POETS' LAUREL
Laurus nobilis

Height: To 18m, but usually much less
Characteristics: Evergreen. A small tree or shrub, broadly conical in outline, with ascending branches. Leaves familiar from culinary use, roughly lanceolate in shape, 5-10cm long, pointed at tip, wedge-shaped at base, hard and leathery, dark green above, paler green below, hairless, with crinkled untoothed margins; highly aromatic if crushed; petiole dark reddish, 5-10mm. Separate male and female flowers; pale creamy yellow in both sexes, reddish in bud, opening to become about 1cm across, borne in pairs at leaf bases. Flowering period April-May. Fruit a globose berry, 0.6-1.2cm diameter, green becoming black.
Range and habitat: Native to Mediterranean region, but cultivated in warmer parts of UK and northern Europe, often as pot shrub.
Similar species: Portuguese Laurel has similar leaves but they are toothed, and the flowers are quite different.

twig with male flowers

fruit

male flowers

female flowers

habit

AVOCADO
Persea americana

Height: To 9m, more in natural habitat
Characteristics: Evergreen. Small tree or bush with rounded outline. Aromatic. Leaves 12-18cm long, ovate, pointed, untoothed, leathery, glabrous, dark green above, paler bluish below. Flowers in short spikes, creamy-yellow. Fruit familiar in cultivated form as green, pitted 'Avocado pear'.
Range and habitat: Probably native to tropical America; widely cultivated in southern Europe, and infrequently in warm conditions further north.
Similar species: None.

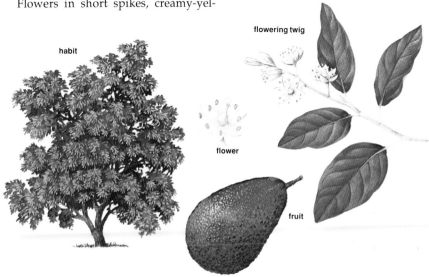

habit

flowering twig

flower

fruit

ORIENTAL SWEET GUM
Liquidambar orientalis
Height: To 8m
Characteristics: Deciduous. A bush or small tree with a dense bushy crown. Bark orange-brown, cracking into flakes. Foliage broadly similar to that of Sweet Gum, but leaves hairless below and rather shinier; petiole shorter than Sweet Gum (3-4cm compared to 10-15cm), and very slender. Flowers generally similar, produced in May.
Range and habitat: Originally from the Middle East and western Asia, but now planted widely though sparingly for ornament. Cultivated commercially for the production of the resinous liquid storax from under the bark.
Similar species: Other *Liquidambar* species, distinguished as detailed, and maples.

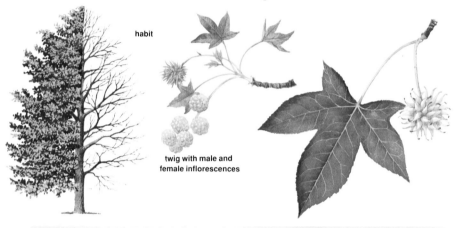

habit

twig with male and
female inflorescences

SWEET GUM
Liquidambar styraciflua
Height: Up to 30m, usually less
Characteristics: Deciduous. A medium-sized tree, conical in outline, becoming domed with age. Bole short, bark grey, becoming cracked and fissured. Leaves maple-like in general shape, but borne alternately; palmate, 3-lobed on younger trees, but 5 or 7 lobed on older trees, green and shiny above, paler below with white hairs in leaf axils; well-known for beautiful autumn red colour, though variable in colour and time. Flowers rare, males and females separate; male flowers small globes in short spike, green-yellow; female flowers in form of ball of yellow-green stigmas, c. 1cm. diameter. Fruit spherical, spiky, persisting through winter.
Range and habitat: Native to south and east USA , widely planted through north-west Europe for ornament in parks and gardens.
Similar species: Oriental Sweet Gum and maples, which differ in their opposite leaves and very different flowers and fruit.

WITCH HAZEL
Hamamelis mollis
Height: To 6m
Characteristics: Deciduous. A shrub or occasionally small tree. The branches are spreading, usually from close to the base, young wood downy. Leaves ovate, rather like Common Hazel, borne alternately, shortly-pointed, rounded at base, with toothed margins; petiole short (0.5-1cm), with large stipules that soon fall. The flowers appear in late winter, long before the leaves (they are mainly planted because they flower so early); they are distinctive in structure, with 4 long, narrow strap-shaped yellow petals, and a calyx of 4 shiny brown sepals; they are borne in small clusters, with very short flower stalks.
Range and habitat: Several species are planted, of which none are native to Europe. *H. mollis* originates from China. They are planted widely in gardens and parks throughout.
Similar species: Two other spring flowering species, and hybrids, are regularly planted, while the autumn flowering *H. virginiana* is less common.

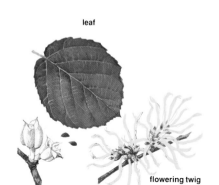

leaf

fruit

flowering twig

89

leafy twig

fruit

flowering twig

PERSIAN IRONWOOD
Parrotia persica
Height: 8-15m
Characteristics: Deciduous. A small tree, spreading from a short bole, with large level or ascending lower branches, sparse upper branches. Bark greyish, flaking in patches revealing pink or yellow. Buds purplish-black and hairy. Leaves roughly ovate or circular, 10-20cm long, with margin wavy and shallowly and irregularly toothed; glabrous and glossy green above, slightly paler below with brownish

habit

pubescence, becoming hairless with age. Veins strongly marked, petiole short and hairy. Flowers bisexual, borne in late winter, long before leaves open, in bunches, mainly of red stamens; fruit in clusters of erect capsules.
Range and habitat: Native to Caucasus area, frequently planted in parks and gardens for early-flowering and attractive bark.
Similar species: None.

PITTOSPORUM
Pittosporum tenuifolium

Height: To 12m, usually less

Characteristics: A small tree or bush, finely-branched, sometimes with short stout bole. Bark dark grey, smooth; twigs finely pubescent when young, purplish-brown at first. Leaves oblong to elliptical, usually 4-6cm long, 2-3cm wide but may be much larger, borne alternately; margins untoothed, but strongly waved and crinkled, with blade bright pale green above with a strongly-marked paler midrib, blade paler below, rather whitish. Petiole short, whitish green. Flowers borne in leaf axils in May, solitary or in small groups; petals deep red-purple, forming small cup-shaped flowers (about 5-8mm in diameter) with outwardly-curving tips, fragrant especially in the evening. Fruit a small almost spherical capsule.

Range and habitat: Native of New Zealand, but now widely planted in gardens and parks for its foliage; commonest in western and coastal areas.

Similar species: *P. crassifolium* is similar, with longer-stalked paler flowers.

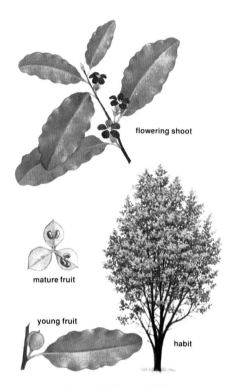

flowering shoot

mature fruit

young fruit

habit

WHITE HOLLY
OR MOCK ORANGE
Pittosporum undulatum

Height: To 20m, usually less

Characteristics: Evergreen. A small conical-triangular tree. Young twigs green. Leaves ovate-lanceolate, pointed, up to 15cm long, rather dark shiny green above, paler below, hairless; margins wavy, untoothed, petiole short or absent. Flowers creamy white, very fragrant, in few-flowered branched inflorescences, produced in May-June; fruit is a small roughly spherical capsule, orange when ripe.

Range and habitat: Native to southeast Australia, cultivated throughout southern Europe in gardens and parks.

Similar species: *P. tobira* is similar, but with rounded leaves, and short-stalked clusters of yellower flowers.

flowering shoot

habit

fruit

ORIENTAL PLANE
Platanus orientalis
Height: To 30m
Characteristics: Deciduous. A medium-large conical or irregularly-domed tree, becoming wide-spreading with age, with lower limbs often resting on the ground; trunk often covered with large burrs. Bark smooth and pale brown, but flaking continually to reveal irregular-shaped patches of yellow below. Leaves palmate with 5 (to 7) lobes, deeply cut, up to 18cm long and as broad; angles between lobes very narrow, central lobe longer than remainder; yellowish-green glossy above, slightly paler below. Petiole long, to about 5cm, with swollen reddish base. Male and female flowers separate; males occur as groups of yellowish spherical flowers, about 1cm diameter; female flowers in groups of 2-6 globose mauve heads; this elongates in fruit, and the large spiny balls hang down on long stalks through the winter.
Range and habitat: Native to southeast Europe; planted widely elsewhere.
Similar species: London Plane.

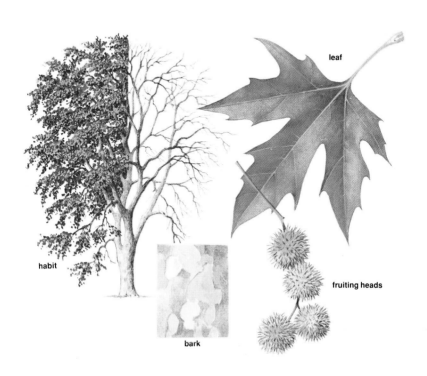

habit

bark

leaf

fruiting heads

male catkins

leaf

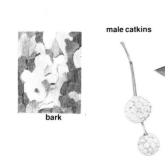

bark

female catkins

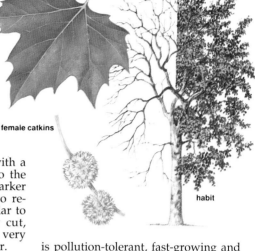

habit

LONDON PLANE
Platanus x hispanica
Height: To 45m
Characteristics: A domed tree, with a long trunk reaching well up into the crown. Bark dark grey-brown, (darker than in Oriental Plane) flaking to reveal yellow patches. Leaves similar to Oriental Plane, but less deeply cut, with wider angles between lobes, very variable. Flowers and fruit similar.
Range and habitat: Origins obscure, though probably of hybrid origin, first noticed in France about 1650. Now very widely planted as street tree, as it

is pollution-tolerant, fast-growing and able to withstand poor management.
Similar species: Oriental Plane. Leaf shape and bark colour are the best features to look at.

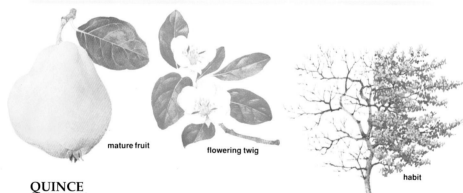

mature fruit

flowering twig

habit

QUINCE
Cydonia oblonga
Height: To 6m, usually less
Characteristics: A rounded and bushy shrub. Bark mid-brown, streaked with orange. Twigs woolly-downy when young, green becoming brown. Leaves 6-15cm long ovate-rectangular, with untoothed margins; upper surface shiny, lower surface paler and downy; petiole 1-2cm, downy, channelled, reddish. Stipules present, persisting. Flowers bisexual, borne singly in leaf axils, bowl-shaped, about 2-4cm diameter, in May; petals pink or white,

longer than the sepals; 5 free styles in centre, anthers numerous. Fruit pear-shaped or spherical, variable in size according to variety from 2-3cm to 8-12cm long, green when young, becoming yellow and sweet-smelling.
Range and habitat: Native to south-west Asia, but widely planted throughout Europe.
Similar species: Medlar is similar, with white flowers with sepals longer than petals.

WILLOW-LEAVED PEAR
Pyrus salicifolia
Height: To 10m, usually less
Characteristics: A bush or small tree. Main branches horizontal, twigs pendulous, white-downy; common cultivated weeping form is *'pendula'*. Leaves narrowly lanceolate, pointed, 4-9cm long, 1-2cm wide, untoothed, greyish and downy on both sides at first, but upper surface becoming glossier with age; overall impression of tree is silvery-grey. Flowers white, c. 2cm in diameter, occurring with leaves in April-May, sepals wooly. Fruit small, globular or pear-shaped, 2-3cm long, green then brown.
Range and habitat: Native of western Asia; commonly cultivated in parks and gardens, especially as var. *pendula*.
Similar species: Distinctive.

fruiting twig

flower

habit

flowering twig

PLYMOUTH PEAR
Pyrus cordata
Height: To 8m
Characteristics: A shrub or small tree. Branches spreading at right angles to slender, often short, trunk, producing a dense bushy shrub. Twigs purplish-brown, usually hairless, spiny. Leaves small compared to other pears, 2-5cm long, ovate, rounded or heart-shaped, with a finely-toothed margin; densely hairy when young, but becoming glossy above paler below with age; petiole 2-3cm long. Flowers appear with leaves, in April, similar to other pears, but smaller (12-18mm diameter, individual petals c. 6-8mm long), white, sometimes pinkish outside. Fruit small (1-1.5cm long) rounded or pear-shaped, covered with lenticels, green becoming reddish.
Range and habitat: An uncommon and local species of woods and hedgerows of the western edge of Europe, from south-west England southwards.
Similar species: Other pears, but size of all parts and fruit shape are key features.

habit

fruiting twig

flowering twig

WILD PEAR
Pyrus pyraster
Height: To 20m
Characteristics: A small-medium, rounded tree, with ascending or spreading branches that are usually spiny. Twigs grey-brown, hairless. Leaves 3-7cm long, elliptical to almost circular, rather thin, hairy at first but glabrous when mature; petiole 3-7cm long. Flowers appear with leaves in April, very similar to Cultivated Pear: petals pure white, flower diameter 2-3.5cm; fruit rounded to pear-shaped, up to 3.5cm long, covered with lenticels, greenish becoming yellow-brown or black; sepals persistent on fruit.
Range and habitat: Occurs through much of south and west Europe, usually singly in woods, scrub and hedges; rare in UK. Very variable, with several types and hybrids occurring.
Similar species: Other pears, especially Common Pear.

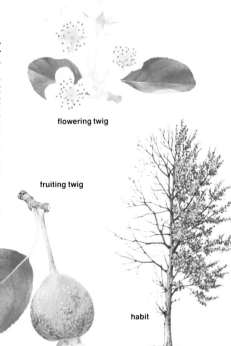

flowering twig

fruiting twig

habit

94

COMMON PEAR
OR CULTIVATED PEAR
Pyrus communis
Height: To 20m, usually less
Characteristics: Deciduous. Familiar as the pear of cultivation, occurring in numerous different forms and varieties. Origins are complex and uncertain, probably arising as a hybrid in cultivation. Generally very similar to Wild Pear, but differs mainly in that Common Pear is not spiny, and its twigs are reddish-brown, sometimes downy when young but becoming very shiny and smooth quickly. Leaves oval to elliptical, not normally rounded or heart-shaped. Fruit distinctive as the familiar edible pear.
Range and habitat: Cultivated throughout much of Europe, except in very dry areas or more northerly regions. Frequently found naturalised or semi-naturalised.
Similar species: Most similar to Wild Pear, with differences as described.

habit

fruiting twig

flowering twig

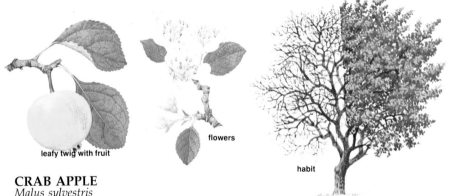

leafy twig with fruit

flowers

habit

CRAB APPLE
Malus sylvestris
Height: To 10m
Characteristics: Deciduous. A shrub or small tree, with bushy spreading, usually thorny, branches. Bark grey-brown, becoming fissured and scaly with age. Leaves variable, ovate to elliptic, sometimes almost circular, 4-8cm long, with a wedge-shaped or rounded base, and a short point at the tip; margins toothed, upper surface mid-green, paler below, hairless when mature; petiole 1.5-3cm long. Flowers white, often strongly flushed with pink, 3-4cm in diameter, appearing with the leaves in April-May in small clusters. Fruit the familiar 'crab apple', almost spherical, 2.5-3cm diameter, greenish becoming yellower, persisting well after leaf fall.
Range and habitat: Common and widespread in woods, hedgerows and scrub.
Similar species: Other apples are most similar.

95

JAPANESE HYBRID APPLE
Malus x floribunda
Height: To 10m, usually less
Characteristics: Deciduous. One of a large number of apple cultivars that are grown primarily for their displays of flowers, rather than for fruit. Produces an extraordinary profusion of flowers in spring, and this alone can often serve to identify it. The buds are deep pink, and the flowers open paler pink, almost white inside. The fruit are crab-apple-like, spherical, 2-3cm in diameter, yellow. Other widely-grown ornamentals include Chinese Crab-apple, *M. spectabilis*, Siberian Crab Apple, *M. baccata*, and the Magdeburg Apple, *M. x magdeburgensis*.
Range and habitat: None are native species, and their occurrence is confined to parks and gardens, where they are common and widespread.
Similar species: Wild Crab Apple.

flowers

fruit

habit

CULTIVATED APPLE

Malus domestica, or *M. sylvestris* ssp. *mitis*

Height: To 15m

Characteristics: The familiar apple tree of gardens and orchards. Its origins are unclear, though it is clearly closely-related to the wild Crab Apple, and shares many characteristics with it. Occurs in numerous named varieties, which differ most in the appearance and taste of their fruit. When in flower, and/or in an uncultivated situation, it can be distinguished from Crab Apple in that it is spineless, whereas Crab Apple is frequently spiny; leaves are similar, though often distinctly larger, and they remain hairy beneath to maturity; flowers similar, often larger, but the sepals and flower stalks are downy or hairy. Fruit very familiar, highly variable but always larger than Crab Apple, and longer than stalk.

Range and habitat: Cultivated throughout, and often found naturalised or as relict of cultivation.

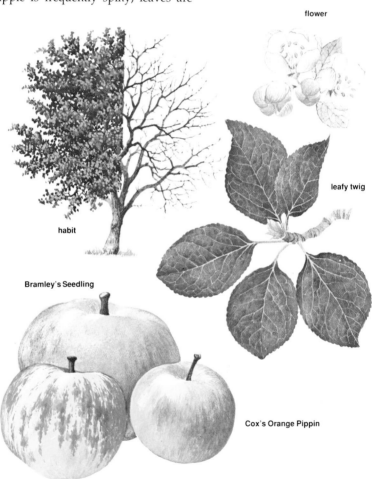

flower

leafy twig

habit

Bramley's Seedling

Cox's Orange Pippin

James Grieve

flowers

leaf

fruit

ROWAN OR MOUNTAIN ASH
Sorbus aucuparia
Height: To 20m
Characteristics: Deciduous. A familiar and graceful tree, medium-sized or small, with few ascending branches producing an ovoid crown. Bark smooth or slightly ridged, grey to silver. Twigs grey or slightly purple. Leaves are pinnate, with 5-8 pairs of leaflets, and a terminal one; leaflets 3-6cm long, oblong-lanceolate, sharply toothed, hairy only when young, mid-green above, paler below; overall leaf length 15-22cm; main leaf stalk round, grooved between leaflets. Flowers occur in May, in rounded heads, with numerous individual flowers each c. 1cm diameter, creamy-white, on woolly pedicels. Fruit more familiar: bunches of bright red globose-ovoid berries, each 7-10mm long, pendulous.
Range and habitat: Widespread and common throughout, especially in mountain areas, both in woods and in open country.
Similar species: True Service Tree, and other rowans.

TRUE SERVICE TREE
Sorbus domestica
Height: To 20m
Characteristics: Deciduous tree with a strong trunk and a domed crown. Leaves pinnate, with 6-10 pairs of leaflets, each 3-6cm long; margins of leaflets sharply double-toothed towards tip. Flowers in creamy-white clusters. Fruit distinctive, large, 2-3cm long, pear-shaped or oval, greenish or brownish. **Range and habitat:** Native of southern Europe; planted further north in parks. **Similar species:** The rowans.

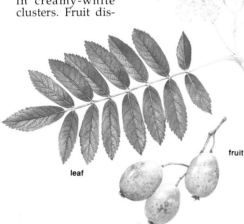

flower

leaf

fruit

habit

98

SARGENT'S ROWAN
Sorbus sargentiana
Height: To 10m
Characteristics: Deciduous. A very similar tree to the European Mountain Ash, and sometimes confused with it. It differs in a number of relatively small details. It is a broader tree, usually with thicker shoots; the twigs are dark brown, and the buds are distinctive in being large, (up to 1.5cm long), glossy, deep red and very resinous. The leaves are similar to those of Mountain Ash, often larger, with more lanceolate long-pointed leaflets, of which the end pair point forwards to overlap the single terminal leaflet. Flowers and fruits generally similar to Mountain Ash; the inflorescence has numerous white hairs. Autumn colour is strong golden or reddish.
Range and habitat: A Chinese species, widely planted in gardens and parks, especially for its foliage and berries. Often grafted onto Mountain Ash. **Similar species:** Other rowans.

leaf

fruit

WILD SERVICE TREE
Sorbus torminalis
Height: To 25m
Characteristics: Spreading or oval-shaped tree; bark brown to greyish, with fine fissures, bark of twigs shiny brown. Buds globose, shiny green; leaves distinctly shaped, with 3-5 dee- ply-incised teeth on each side, green then red in autumn. Flowers in clusters, white, about 10-15mm in diameter, with woolly pedicels, May-June. 2 styles. Fruit ovoid, 12-18mm in diameter, brown and finely-dotted, ripening September.
Range and habitat: Mainly a woodland or scrub tree, usually on heavy soils. Widespread, though not in the far north. Occasionally planted ornamentally.
Similar species: No other *Sorbus* species has the combination of deeply-cut leaves, and brownish fruit.

habit

flowering twig

fruit

WHITEBEAM
Sorbus aria
Height: To 25m, usually less
Characteristics: Deciduous. A medium-sized tree. Bark smooth grey, becoming ridged. Branches ascending. Leaves ovate or elliptical, 6-12cm long, bluntly pointed at the tip, dull green above and densely white-downy below; margins toothed, petiole 1-2cm. Flowers produced in May-June in heads of creamy-white flowers, similar to other Sorbus species. Berries ovoid, red when ripe, though not as bright or prolific as Rowan.
Range and habitat: Common and widespread throughout much of west and central Europe, especially on calcareous soils; planted in parks, streets and gardens.
Similar species: *Sorbus graeca* and *S. rupicola* are the most similar.

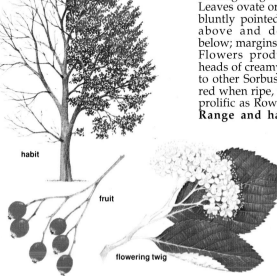

habit

fruit

flowering twig

SORBUS GRAECA
Height: To 4m
Characteristics: This is the south-east European equivalent of *S. rupicola*, easily confused with it and with Common Whitebeam. Very similar to *S. rupicola* in most respects, though there are 9-11 pairs of lateral veins in the leaf; the marginal leaf teeth are even and not curved; the leaves are rather leathery.
Range and habitat: Rocky areas, especially limestone.
Similar species: Whitebeam and *S. rupicola*.

SORBUS AUSTRIACA
Height: To 8m, often less
Characteristics: Generally like a small Whitebeam, and closely related to it. Differs in that the leaves are more distinctly lobed, with cuts extending about a third of the way to the midrib; the lobes themselves are toothed. The leaf undersurface is greyish-white, though usually less densely woolly than Whitebeam.
Range and habitat: Hills and mountains in central Europe.

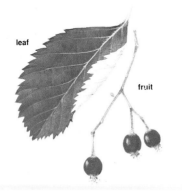

leaf

fruit

leaf

fruit

100

SWEDISH WHITEBEAM
Sorbus intermedia
Height: To 15m
Characteristics: Deciduous. Another of the many confusing Sorbus species, roughly intermediate between Whitebeam and Mountain Ash in character. Bark smooth greyish, sometimes fissured; twigs pubescent at first, becoming hairy. Leaves ovate-elliptic, wedge-shaped to rounded at base; upper half is increasingly deeply-toothed from apex, while lower half is lobed, with deepest lobes reaching up to a third of the way to the midrib (occasionally more pronounced on vigorous shoots); leaves green above, yellowish-grey woolly below.
Range and habitat: Native to Scandinavia and north Germany; widely planted as a street tree elsewhere.
Similar species: *Sorbus austriaca*.

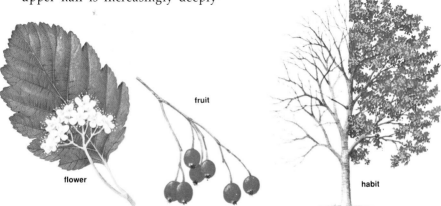

flower

fruit

habit

habit

flowering twig

fruit

SERVICE TREE OF FONTAINEBLEAU
Sorbus x latifolia
Height: To 20m
Characteristics: Deciduous. Thought to have arisen as a hybrid between Whitebeam and Wild Service Tree, first found in Fontainebleau Forest, France. Similar to other *Sorbus* species, distinguished mainly by its large broad leaves (up to 20cm x 12cm wide), which are ovate-triangular, with two large lobes at the base, tapering to a wedge-shaped base; green above, white-hairy below, toothed all round. Flowers and fruit are typical of the group, except the berries ripen to yellow, with large brown lenticels.
Range and habitat: In woods and on limestone rocks from south Britain southwards; local.
Similar species: Other whitebeams.

101

BASTARD SERVICE TREE
Sorbus hybrida
Height: To 15m
Characteristics: Deciduous. Roughly intermediate between Mountain Ash and Common Whitebeam, from which it may have derived as a hybrid. Leaves pinnately lobed, somewhat variably, but most usually with the basal two pairs of leaflets clearly separated, the remainder together in a decreasingly strongly-lobed block; the pinnae or lobes are toothed towards the tip; the upper surface is mid-green, hairless, the undersurface is densely white-woolly. Flowers and fruit typical in general characteristics: flowers smallish (c. 1cm diameter), creamy-white; fruits 1-1.2cm long, ovoid-globose, bright red with small lenticels.
Range and habitat: Woodlands and open rocky habitats in south and west Scandinavia. Not native in UK.
Similar species: The rowans are most similar, with leaf shape and white leaf undersurface important distinctions.

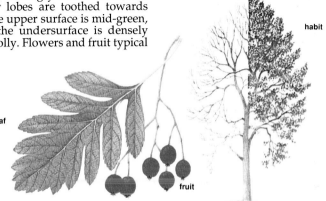

leaf

habit

fruit

SNOWY MESPIL
Amelanchier ovalis

Height: To 5m, usually less
Characteristics: Deciduous. A shrub, or occasionally, a small tree, erect or spreading, usually much-branched. Young twigs woolly with white down, bark blackish. Leaves ovate, 3-5cm long, rounded, pointed, or notched at apex, wedge-shaped at base, coarsely toothed with between 3 and 5 teeth per centimetre; upper surface mid-green, white-woolly below. Flowers bisexual, produced in April-May, in a raceme of 3-8 white flowers, each about 1.5-2cm across. There are 5 free styles in the centre. The fruit is a bluish-black glo-bose-ovoid berry, 0.8-1cm long, which is edible and sweet.

Range and habitat: Not in UK, but widespread throughout much of central Europe in woods, rocky areas and mountains, to 2400m.

Similar species: Other *Amelanchier* species are very similar – a difficult group, with confused naming!

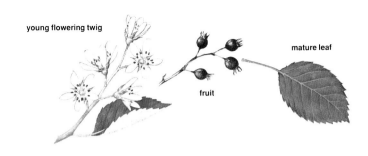

young flowering twig

fruit

mature leaf

102

AMELANCHIER SPICATA

Height: To 4m
Characteristics: Deciduous. A shrub, or very occasionally small tree. Very similar in most respects to Snowy Mespil, above, differing in minor structural details as follows: leaves are similar, but are more finely toothed, with 8-12 teeth per centimetre of margin, and the undersurface is more densely and persistently white-woolly. The flowers are similar, but rather smaller – about 1/2 -2/3rds of the size – while the central 5 styles are fused together at the base rather than free; the tip of the ovary, if examined under a lens, is seen to be hairy in this species (cf. hairless in Snowy Mespil). Fruit similar, but slightly smaller.

Range and habitat: Probably from eastern N. America originally, widely grown in gardens and parks, and occasionally naturalised in hedges and open woodland in central Europe.

Similar species: Other *Amelanchier* species, especially *A. ovalis.*

JUNE BERRY

Amelanchier grandiflora (also known as
A. lamarckii)
Height: To 9m
Characteristics: Deciduous. A shrub or
small tree. Young twigs hairy. Leaves
elliptical to rather heart-shaped, finely-
toothed along the margins at the rate
of 6-12 teeth per centimetre; the leaves
emerge purplish-red and downy, becoming almost hairless and grey-green
as they mature. Flowers in drooping
racemes containing 10-15 large white
flowers, 3.5-4cm across; flower pedicels long, 2-2.5cm. Fruit dark purple,
globose, rather larger than the preced-
ing 2 species, edible and sweet.
Range and habitat: A species of garden origin, un-
known in the wild.
Widely planted in
gardens and parks.
Similar species:
Other *Amelanchiers*.

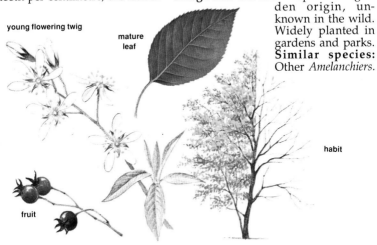

young flowering twig

mature
leaf

habit

fruit

ALLEGHENY SERVICEBERRY OR SNOWY MESPIL

Amelanchier laevis
Height: Up to 20m, usually less
Characteristics: Deciduous. This
species is the subject of most confusion
in naming, having been known as, or
confused with, *A. canadensis*, and *A. lamarckii*, and the nomenclature is still
not fully sorted out. Similar in general
characteristics to *A. ovalis* and *A. spica-
ta*; the leaves are ovate, pointed at the
tip, finely toothed, emerging pinkish-
purple, becoming green, glabrous
throughout; this species is noted for its
autumn foliage colour of rich red and
gold. Fruit small, to 6mm, ovoid, hairless, yellow-green, becoming purplish.
Range and habitat: Probably native to
eastern N. America, though somewhat
confused in origin. Widely planted in
parks, etc., for its autumn colour.
Similar species: Other *Amelanchiers*.

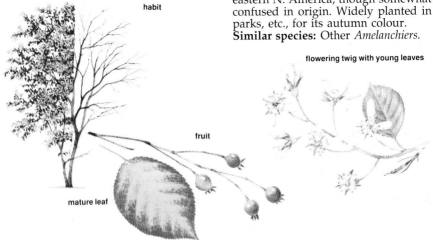

habit

flowering twig with young leaves

fruit

mature leaf

flowering twig

fruit

habit

HIMALAYAN TREE COTONEASTER
Cotoneaster frigidus
Height: To 20m
Characteristics: Deciduous or semi-evergreen. The only common Cotoneaster that grows into a tree. A short-medium tree, with a short trunk, or a series of branches spreading from the base and arching outwards. Bark greyish-brown. Leaves elliptical or oblong, wedge-shaped at base, 6-12cm

104

long, dark green above, white-hairy with dense felt below; margins untoothed, petiole 0.5-1cm. Inflorescence consists of dense cluster of creamy-white flowers, individually 5-8mm, collectively about 5cm in diameter. Fruits are ovoid-globular, red with red flesh, about 5mm long.
Range and habitat: Native to the Himalayas, as the common name indicates, but widely planted in parks and gardens for ornament. Commonest in western areas.
Similar species: Fairly distinctive.

habit

flowering twig

mature fruit

MEDLAR
Mespilus germanica
Height: To 6m
Characteristics: Most commonly a spreading densely-tangled shrub, occasionally a small tree. Sparsely spiny. Young shoots densely hairy. Leaves oblong to broadly lanceolate, 5-15cm long, dull yellowish-green and hairless above, paler with a covering of dense white hairs below; veins strongly impressed, giving a crinkled look to the leaves; margin entire or minutely toothed. Flowers solitary, produced in May, large (3-5cm diameter), white or slightly pink, with numerous reddish anthers; sepals are distinctly longer than petals, persisting after petals fall. Fruit roughly apple-shaped, held within sepals, 2-3cm long.
Range and habitat: Native to southeast Europe and west Asia, but widely naturalised through Europe as far north as south-east England. Cultivated forms are spineless with larger fruit.
Similar species: Quince is somewhat similar.

COCKSPUR THORN

Crataegus crus-galli

Height: To 10m

Characteristics: Deciduous. Bark greybrown, smooth but becoming finely-fissured; twigs purplish and carrying numerous long thorns. Leaves unlike most hawthorns in being unlobed, obovate, 5-8cm long, wedgeshaped at the base, and widest above the middle, green and hairless on both sides; margins toothed except at base. Flowers as most hawthorns, in a lax cluster of 6 or so white flowers, each 1-1.5cm diameter, produced in May. Fruit ovoid, red, to 1cm, persisting through winter.

Range and habitat: Native of northeast USA, frequently planted in parks, gardens and streets, especially for its rich orange autumn foliage.

Similar species: None.

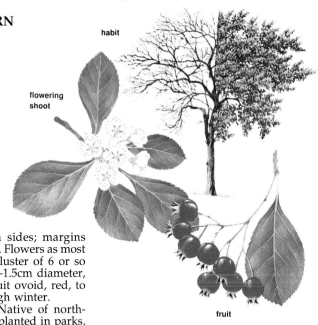

habit

flowering shoot

fruit

flowering shoot

fruit

habit

MIDLAND HAWTHORN

Crataegus laevigata

Height: To 10m, usually less

Characteristics: Deciduous. A typical Hawthorn, differing from Common Hawthorn only in relatively minor details. Twigs sparsely spiny. Leaves ovate-triangular with 3-5 lobes which are not deeply incised (reaching less than halfway to the midrib) and sometimes absent altogether; general appearance more rounded than Common Hawthorn. Flowers and fruit similar to Common Hawthorn, though rather more sparsely produced, except that there are 2-3 styles, visible in flower and fruit, not 1. Flowers May-June.

Range and habitat: Widespread in central Europe, local in England, usually in woodland – in England, a plant of old woodlands, rather than scrub or open land.

Similar species: Other hawthorns, especially Common Hawthorn.

habit

fruit

flowering shoot

COMMON HAWTHORN
Crataegus monogyna
Height: To 15m
Characteristics: Deciduous. A very familiar shrub or small tree, common almost everywhere. Bole simple or branched, bark brownish, usually cracking into rectangular plates. Twigs bear many thorns. Leaves triangular-ovate, 1-1.5 times as long as broad, reaching 3-4.5cm long; deeply divided into 3-5 lobes, with the divisions often reaching more than half way to the midrib; individual lobes pointed, slightly toothed; upper surface shiny green, paler and matt below, with tufts of hairs in vein axils; petiole often pinkish. Flowers occur in rounded clusters of 10-18 flowers, individually 1-1.5cm diameter, white or pink; there is only one central style. Fruit is a red globose berry, the well-known 'haw'.
Range and habitat: Very common and widespread in open and semi-shaded habitats, uncommon in dense woodland. Especially common in hedges, where it is often planted.
Similar species: Other Hawthorns, especially *C. laevigata* and *C. calycina*.

AZAROLE
Crataegus azarolus
Height: To 8m
Characteristics: Deciduous. Similar to other hawthorns, but distinctive by virtue of its fruits. The only hawthorn likely to be found cultivated in orchards. Leaves ovate-triangular, to 5cm long, divided into 3-5 narrow lanceolate lobes which are markedly forward-pointing; the divisions reach more than halfway to the midrib; the base is wedge-shaped, sometimes spreading down into the petiole.

Flowers typical of the genus. Fruit globose, slightly flattened at base, angled longitudinally, ripening orange; styles 2-3.
Range and habitat: Native to southeast Europe; more widely cultivated in warmer areas especially France. Rare in Britain.
Similar species: Other hawthorns.

flowering shoot

fruit

habit

CRATAEGUS CALYCINA
Height: To 10m
Characteristics: Deciduous. Very simi-

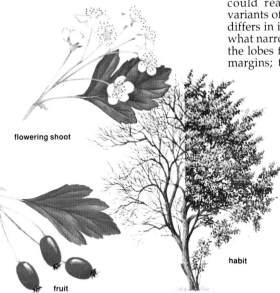

flowering shoot

fruit

lar to Common Hawthorn, and confused with it where the two species overlap in range. The two species are essentially extremes of variation, and could reasonably be considered as variants of the same species. *C. calycina* differs in its leaf shape, which is somewhat narrower, less deeply-lobed, with the lobes finely toothed all around the margins; the base is strongly wedge-shaped, and the petiole is about half as long as the blade. Flowers slightly larger, 1.5-2cm diameter, with 1 style. Fruit similar to the haw, slightly larger (1-1.5cm long), darker red, with more erect persistent sepals.
Range and habitat: Not in UK. A shade-tolerant species of woods in central and eastern Europe.
Similar species: Common Hawthorn, and other hawthorns.

habit

PEACH
Prunus persica
Height: Up to 6m
Characteristics: Deciduous. A rounded bush or small tree when grown free, though most often seen as an orchard tree, grown as an espalier, or against a wall. Leaves narrow oblong-lanceolate or elliptical, 5-15cm long, long-pointed, wedge-shaped at base; margins finely-toothed, smooth green above, paler

below; petiole 1-2cm long. Flowers short-stalked, in ones or twos, appearing, often abundantly, before the leaves open; petals pink, sometimes white or dark pink, 1-2cm long. Fruit is the familiar peach – spherical, velvety, 4-8cm diameter, borne on a very short stalk, yellowish suffused with red, with a large single-seeded stone, edible and juicy. The smooth-skinned nectarine is the same species.
Range and habitat: Cultivated commercially in southern Europe, more sparingly in gardens further north.
Similar species: Almond, in flower.

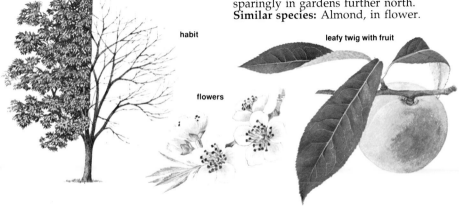

habit

leafy twig with fruit

flowers

ALMOND
Prunus dulcis
Height: Up to 8m
Characteristics: Deciduous. Closely related to Peach, and similar superficially. A bush or small tree, broad and rounded when mature. Bark blackish, deeply-cracked into rectangles. Branches normally spineless in cultivated trees. Leaves are oblong-lanceolate, 5-12cm, long-pointed, usually broadest at or below the middle, bright green above, paler below; margins finely toothed, petiole c. 2cm long. Flowers bright pink, occasionally white, produced abundantly before the leaves, often as early as February; petals 1.5-2.5cm long. Fruit is ovoid, distinctly flattened, 3.5-6cm long, velvety grey-green, containing a single almond.
Range and habitat: Widely cultivated commercially in southern Europe, and locally further north.
Similar species: Peach.

flowers

leafy twig with fruit

habit

APRICOT
Prunus armeniaca
Height: To 10m, usually less
Characteristics: Deciduous. A bush or small rounded tree. Bark greyish-brown, becoming finely cracked. Branches twisted and wavy. Leaves ovate or almost circular, abruptly pointed, 5-10cm long and almost as broad, squared off or heart-shaped at base, mid to dark green; margin with small sharp teeth, petiole 2-4cm, reddish. Flowers solitary or paired, pale pink or white, about 2cm diameter, short-stalked, appearing in March-April, before the leaves emerge. Fruit globose, 4-7cm diameter, downy, ripening to reddish-orange. Edible and sweet.
Range and habitat: Native to central and east Asia; widely cultivated as a crop in southern Europe, more sparingly further north.
Similar species: Fruit and leaf shape distinctive.

habit

flowers

leafy twig with fruit

CHERRY PLUM OR MYROBALAN

Prunus cerasifera

Height: To 8m

Characteristics: Deciduous. A shrub or small rounded tree. Bark dark brown, with rows of lenticels, twigs very numerous, fine, green then brown and shiny, usually with few or no spines. Leaves ovate or oblong, to 5cm long, shiny mid-green above, matt and paler below with veins downy; margins with regular rounded teeth, petiole purplish-green, 1cm, grooved. Flowers white or pale pink, solitary but with several occurring close together, 1.5-2cm diameter, pedicels 1-1.5cm long. Fruit globose, smooth, red when ripe, often with a touch of yellow or green, 2-3cm diameter, edible. Flowers in March, and fruits early, in July.

Range and habitat: Native of southeast Europe and adjacent Asia, widely cultivated for fruit. Var *pissardii* has dark reddish leaves and pink flowers, often cultivated for ornament.

Similar species: Other *Prunus* species.

habit

leafy twig with fruit

flowers

SLOE OR BLACKTHORN

Prunus spinosa

Height: To 6m

Characteristics: A familiar thickly-branched spiny shrub or very small tree, that puts out numerous suckers. Bark dark brown. Leaves ovate, usually broadest above the middle, 2-5cm long, dull green and smooth above, paler and downy on the veins below; margins with small rounded teeth, petiole c. 1cm long. Flowers solitary, but close together on the branches, produced just before leaves, often strikingly abundant in March-April; individual flowers white, 1-1.5cm diameter, stamens red. Fruit is well-known sloe, globose, 1-1.5cm diameter, blue-black with distinct bloom on surface, fleshy but astringent.

Range and habitat: Very common and widespread in UK and most of Europe, especially in hedges and scrub.

Similar species: Plum and Bullace.

habit

leafy twig with fruit

flowers

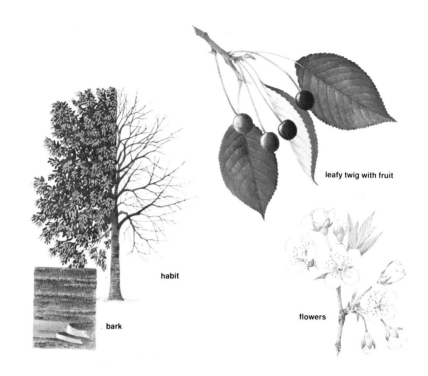

leafy twig with fruit

habit

bark

flowers

110

GEAN OR WILD CHERRY
Prunus avium

Height: To 30m

Characteristics: Deciduous. A medium-large conical to broad-crowned tree, usually with a well-developed trunk. Bark shiny reddish-brown, duller in parts, becoming fissured; young twigs smooth. Leaves ovate to oblong-ovate, 10-15cm long, with a long tapering point, dull green above, paler and downy on the veins below; margins have regular forward-projecting teeth, petiole is 3-5cm long with reddish glands at the blade end. Flowers appear with or just before the leaves, in April-May, usually in clusters of 2-6, white, individually 1.5-2.5cm across, on long pedicels. Fruit globose, 1-2cm long, red to almost black, usually sweet and fleshy.

Range and habitat: Widespread and common through most of Europe, especially on clay and limestone soils. Cultivated cherries derive from this species.

Similar species: Sour Cherry is most similar.

PLUM AND BULLACE
Prunus domestica
Height: To 10m

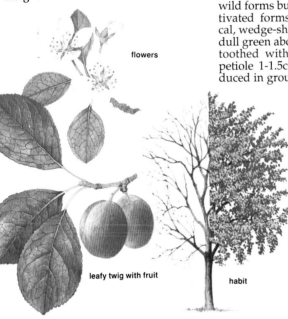

flowers

leafy twig with fruit

habit

Characteristics: Deciduous. A shrub or small tree, suckering freely; twigs often abundant and tangled, dull, spiny in wild forms but usually spineless in cultivated forms. Leaves obovate-elliptical, wedge-shaped at base, smooth and dull green above, paler below; margins toothed with regular rounded teeth, petiole 1-1.5cm, downy. Flowers produced in groups of 2-3 with the leaves, white or greenish-tinged, 1.5-2.5cm diameter on 1-2cm pedicels. Fruit variable: globose to ovoid, pendulous, 2-7cm long, blue-black to red. Bullace (ssp. *institia*) has whiter flowers, smaller fruit and downier twigs than pure wild plum.
Range and habitat: Common and widespread, both as native and escape.

SOUR CHERRY
OR DWARF CHERRY
Prunus cerasus
Height: To 6m
Characteristics: Deciduous. A shrub or very small tree. Generally very like Gean, but much smaller with – as the name suggests – more acid fruits. It is grown commercially for the production of Morello, or sour, cherries for preserving. Differs mainly in being smaller in stature, freely-suckering; leaves glossier above, rather narrower than those of Gean, becoming hairless below. Flowers rather smaller, 1.2-1.8cm diameter, in clusters of 2-6, white or pink. The fruit is very similar in appearance, sometimes paler in colour, but acidic to the taste even when fully ripe.
Range and habitat: Native to south-west Asia, but widely planted for its fruit, or for ornament in double-flowered forms. Occasionally naturalised.
Similar species: Gean is most similar.

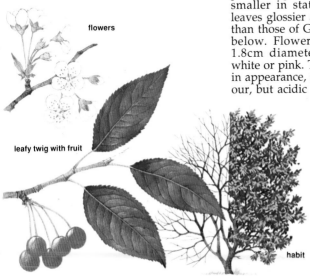

flowers

leafy twig with fruit

habit

SARGENT'S CHERRY
Prunus sargentii
Height: To 25m in its native habitat, usually rather less in cultivation
Characteristics: Deciduous. Generally similar in overall features to the common native cherries, but differing in several distinct features. Shape variable, and often grafted onto Gean stock to improve growth. Bark purple-brown, with horizontal raised lines of lenticels. Leaves oblong-obovate with a long point, petiole grooved and deep red, to 4cm long. Flowers borne in dense clusters, individually rosy-pink, about 3-4cm diameter, produced in mid-April, usually just before the leaves. Fruit ovoid, dark crimson to black, but rarely seen in cultivation.
Range and habitat: Native to Japan and the Sakhalin Islands, but widely used in cultivation as a street tree, and in parks and gardens.
Similar species: Japanese Cherry.

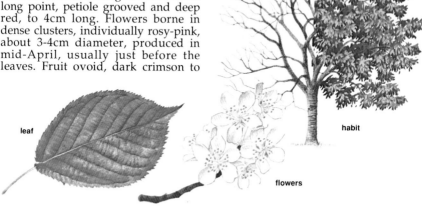

leaf

flowers

habit

112

JAPANESE CHERRY
Prunus serrulata
Height: To 15m, but usually much less
Characteristics: A very difficult species to characterise adequately, because of its origins – originated in China, proliferated in Japan, then introduced to Europe in a number of forms, subsequently developed. Thus it is a hugely variable tree. Its key characteristics are its large (12-20cm x 5-10cm) broadly ovate or obovate leaves, which are sharply toothed, and which turn pink and gold in autumn. Tree shape is very variable. Flowers in clusters, single or double, 2-4cm across, white or, more commonly, pink.
Range and habitat: Introduced, and now planted very widely under numerous named forms in gardens, parks, streets, and landscaping schemes.
Similar species: Sargent's Cherry, Yoshino Cherry.

'Amanogawa' leaf

'Amanogawa' habit

'Kanzan' bark

'Kanzan' flowers

YOSHINO CHERRY
Prunus x *yedoensis*
Height: To 10m
Characteristics: Deciduous. A tree of garden origin, believed to have arisen in Japan as a result of a hybrid between *Prunus speciosa* and *P. subhirtella*. The flowers are said to be particularly prone to damage by bullfinches where they are common. Twigs downy at first, becoming glabrous as they mature. Leaves ovate, pointed, glossy above, paler and pubescent on veins beneath, slightly folded at base; margins with uneven teeth, each fine-pointed. A highly floriferous tree, producing an abundance of short-stalked flowers, in groups of 4-6; pink in bud then opening almost white, broad and flat (3-4cm across), petals deeply notched. Fruit ovoid, red and yellow, but rarely seen in cultivation.
Range and habitat: Introduced. Very commonly planted in parks, gardens, streets, landscaping schemes etc. for its spring flowers, though rather a dull tree for the rest of the year.
Similar species: Cherries of Japanese origin, especially Japanese Cherry.

leaf

flowers

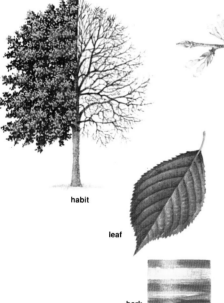

flowers

habit

leaf

bark

SPRING CHERRY
Prunus subhirtella
Height: To 12m
Characteristics: Deciduous. A cherry with confusing names, since the commonest variety of this species – cv. autumnalis – flowers through the winter. Flowers small, before the leaves, pale pink, with notched or fringed petal tips.
Range and habitat: Widely planted in gardens and parks, especially as cv. autumnalis, the commonest winter-flowering cherry.

TIBETAN CHERRY
Prunus serrula
Characteristics: Like Spring Cherry, but with bark blackish, peeling brown; flowers white, with leaves. Moderately commonly planted for ornament.

SAINT LUCIE'S CHERRY
Prunus mahaleb
Height: To 10m
Characteristics: Deciduous. A shrub, or, rarely, a small tree. Bark greyish-brown, young twigs glandular-hairy, branches spreading. Leaves broadly ovate to almost circular, small (3-7cm long), finely toothed, glandular along the margin, smooth and glossy above, paler below with pubescence along veins. The flowers are produced in April-May, short racemes at the end of short leafy shoots; each flower is small (about 1cm diameter), white, fragrant, with 3-10 flowers in a raceme. Fruit ovoid to spherical, green at first becoming black, bitter and fleshy.
Range and habitat: Not native to UK. A widespread native of central continental Europe, in scrub, open woodland, rough hillsides and other habitats, where it is frequent. Planted elsewhere, including Britain, naturalising occasionally.
Similar species: Bird Cherry.

leafy twig with fruit

flowers

habit

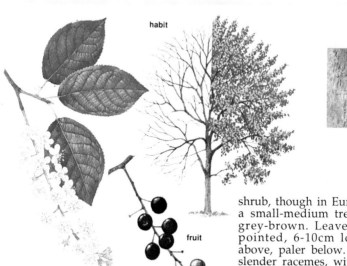

habit

bark

fruit

leafy twig with flowers

BIRD CHERRY
Prunus padus
Height: To 15m, usually less
Characteristics: Deciduous. In Britain, this species usually occurs as a small shrub, though in Europe it may form a small-medium tree. Bark smooth, grey-brown. Leaves elliptic-ovate, pointed, 6-10cm long, dull green above, paler below. Flowers in long slender racemes, with 15-35 flowers, white, produced in May with the leaves. Fruits globose, 6-8mm diameter, black and glossy.
Range and habitat: Widespread both as a native tree and planted for ornament. In UK, rare in the south and east, commoner in the north.
Similar species: Portugal Laurel.

PORTUGAL LAUREL
Prunus lusitanica
Height: To 12m (rarely more)
Characteristics: Evergreen. Shrub or small domed tree with dense branches. Bark black and smooth or slightly scaly. Twigs smooth, often reddish. Leaves ovate to oblong, with rounded base, 8-12cm long, smooth and leathery, upper surface dark glossy green, lower surface paler and yellowish; margin shallowly, regularly toothed, petiole c. 2cm long, red. Flowers in elongated racemes, up to 25cm long, containing up to 100 flowers, each about 1cm diameter, creamy-white, fragrant. Fruit ovoid or globose, shiny, c. 1cm long, becoming black.
Range and habitat: Native of southwest Europe, but very widely planted for ornament, hedging, cover etc., occasionally naturalising.
Similar species: Bird Cherry is deciduous; Cherry Laurel.

habit

flowering shoot

ripening fruit

115

CHERRY LAUREL
Prunus laurocerasus
Height: To 14m, usually less
Characteristics: Evergreen. A shrub or small tree. Leaves oblong-lanceolate, with a short tip, smooth and leathery, dark glossy green above, paler yellowish below; margins barely toothed. Inflorescence an erect spike of 20-30 creamy-white small flowers, in April; fruit ovoid or globose, c. 1cm long, turning blackish when ripe.
Range and habitat: Native to southeast Europe and south-west Asia, but widely planted for ornament, shelter, cover; in UK particularly common in the south-west.
Similar species: Portugal Laurel, though the rounded almost untoothed leaves of Cherry Laurel are distinctive.

flowering shoot

fruit

habit

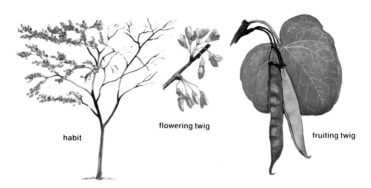

habit

flowering twig

fruiting twig

JUDAS TREE
Cercis siliquastrum
Height: To 10m
Characteristics: Deciduous. A shrub or small tree, with a rounded or irregular crown, frequently with several main stems spreading from the base. Twigs red-brown. Leaves alternately borne, almost circular with a rounded tip and a heart-shaped base, 8-12cm long, untoothed; grey green when young, becoming yellowish-green later above, glaucous below. Flowers are borne in distinctive clusters directly on the old wood or on younger twigs, usually appearing before the leaves; individual flowers pink, pea-flower like, with 6 or so in a cluster; fruits are compressed legumes, 6-10cm long, green then reddish then brown.
Range and habitat: A native of southern Europe and western Asia, though very widely planted in parks and gardens further north for ornament.
Similar species: Flowers and leaves together highly distinctive; the Katsura Tree has similar foliage, but leaves are in opposite pairs.

116

flowering twig

male flower

immature fruit

habit

CAROB TREE
OR LOCUST TREE
Ceratonia siliqua
Height: To 12m
Characteristics: Evergreen. A small-medium tree or shrub, with a densely-leafy crown. Leaves pinnate, with between 2 and 5 pairs of leaflets, but no terminal leaflet; the individual leaflets are obovate, untoothed, mid-green, 3-5cm long, and the rachis is green or brownish. The flowers are produced in a short axillary raceme of tiny greenish petal-less flowers, occasionally produced on old wood; the fruit is a legume, laterally compressed, 10-20cm long, green at first becoming purplish-brown when ripe, pendent. The pods are the source of carob, used as a chocolate substitute, and for fodder.
Range and habitat: Native of parts of Mediterranean Europe, and widely grown in orchards in southern Europe. Not in UK, or the remainder of northern Europe.
Similar species: None. The large-lobed pinnate leaves and long pods, often on the wood, are distinctive.

GOLDEN WREATH
OR WILLOW WATTLE
Acacia cyanophylla
Height: To 10m
Characteristics: A shrub or small tree. Phyllodes (the 'leaves' of *Acacia* species are not true leaves, but flattened petioles without a blade) variable, straight or curved, up to 20cm long, glaucous, with a conspicuous midrib. Inflorescence of large globular yellow heads (1-1.5cm diameter), in pendulous racemes.
Range and habitat: Native to west Australia; widely planted in southern Europe. Not in UK.
Similar species: *A. retinodes* is similar.

legume

phyllodes

habit

flowers

SILVER WATTLE OR MIMOSA
Acacia dealbata
Height: To 30m in good conditions
Characteristics: A medium-sized tree, larger than most *Acacias* grown in Europe. Twigs, young shoots and leaves all covered in silvery-white pubescence. Leaves bipinnate. Inflorescences terminal or axillary, consisting of 20-30 small (5-6mm diameter) bright yellow flower heads, with 30-40 flowers in each.
Range and habitat: Native to southeast Australia, now widely planted and naturalised in southern Europe, and as far north as southern England.
Similar species: None in UK.

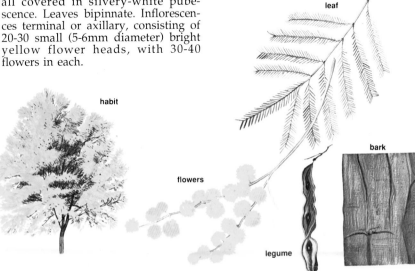

leaf

habit

flowers

bark

legume

habit

phyllodes with inflorescence

legume

118

BLACKWOOD
Acacia melanoxylon

Height: Usually 15m or less, but to 40m in particularly favourable conditions

Characteristics: A tree, with a distinct trunk, conical in shape; bark dark grey-brown, becoming rough and fissured. Branches horizontal or pendulous. Phyllodes are lanceolate to ovate, broader than many species, up to 12cm long, slightly curved, bluntly pointed; dull dark-green in colour, untoothed, with 3-5 almost parallel veins; some leaves may be pinnate, on young trees. The inflorescence consists of a short spike of few globular pale yellow or creamy-white heads, each about 1cm in diameter. Fruit is a compressed, twisted, brownish legume, up to 10cm long.

Range and habitat: A native of southeast Australia and Tasmania, planted widely in southern Europe for its veneer timber ('blackwood'), locally naturalised. Occasional in UK.

Similar species: Other *Acacias* generally similar; details of phyllodes, flowers and pod are significant.

SWAMP WATTLE
Acacia retinodes

Height: To 10m

Characteristics: A small tree or shrub, with a short trunk and smooth greyish bark. Phyllodes variable, but usually linear, 6-15cm long, slightly curved, light green, with a clearly-defined midrib. Flowers produced in short inflorescences, of 5-10 small (4-6mm diameter) pale yellow spherical heads. Flowers in June-July.

Range and habitat: Native to south Australia; widely planted for ornament in southern Europe, as far north as Britain; naturalises occasionally.

Similar species: Golden Wreath is similar, but earlier-flowering, broader-leaved and larger-flowered.

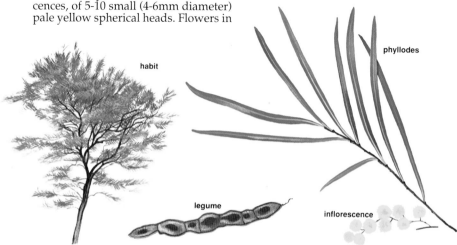

habit

phyllodes

legume

inflorescence

COMMON LABURNUM
Laburnum anagyroides
Height: To 7m

Characteristics: A small tree or shrub, with an open, irregular crown, slender trunk, and few ascending branches. Bark greenish-brown, smooth. Twigs greyish-green with long, silky, closely-pressed hairs. Leaves trifoliate, each leaflet similar: roughly elliptical, 3-8cm long, blunt, greyish-green on both surfaces, but hairy below when young; margin untoothed, petiole 3-6cm long. Flowers familiar: a pendulous, rather loose raceme of numerous golden-yellow pea-like flowers, 10-30cm in total length, produced from late April to early June; corolla golden yellow with brown markings. Seed pod hairy when young, glabrous when mature. Seeds black when ripe. Highly poisonous.

Range and habitat: Native to southern Europe, but very widely planted for ornament in northern Europe, naturalising readily especially on warm dry slopes. Short-lived.

Similar species: Alpine Laburnum or Scotch Laburnum, and the hybrid with Common Laburnum.

ripe fruit

flowering twig

119

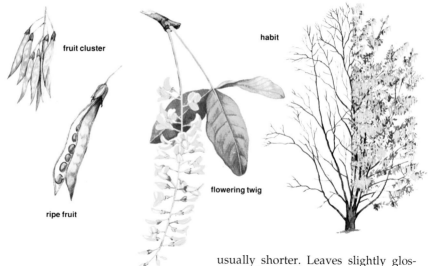

fruit cluster

habit

ripe fruit

flowering twig

ALPINE LABURNUM OR SCOTCH LABURNUM
Laburnum alpinum
Height: To 5m
Characteristics: Similar to Common Laburnum. Green twigs are hairy only when young, glabrous later; trunk usually shorter. Leaves slightly glossier, and virtually hairless on both surfaces. Racemes of flowers longer (to 40cm), slenderer and denser. Flowers later, in June. Pods are hairless, seeds brown not black when ripe.
Range and habitat: Native to southern Europe in mountains; widely planted for ornament; naturalised in Scotland.

PAGODA TREE
Sophora japonica
Height: To 25m in favourable conditions, usually less
Characteristics: Deciduous. Medium-sized tree, with contorted branches and upper trunk. Bark grey-brown, furrowed. Leaves pinnate, to 25cm, with 4-8 pairs of leaflets, and one terminal one, borne alternately. Flowers white or pink, pea-flower-like, in large panicles which are 15-25cm long, produced in late summer. Fruit in the form of a legume pod, greenish, strongly constricted between seeds.
Range and habitat: Native to east Asia, but often planted in parks and gardens, and occasionally naturalised. Mainly southern Europe.
Similar species: Locust Tree.

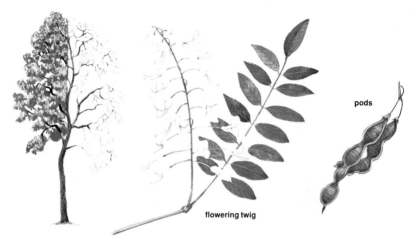

pods

flowering twig

flowering twigs

pods

LOCUST TREE
Robinia pseudacacia
Height: To 25m
Characteristics: Deciduous. A medium sized ovate-conical tree, with a rather open crown; frequently spreads by suckers, forming small thickets around the parent tree. Bark dark brown, becoming greyer and more ridged in older trees. Branches twisted, young twigs reddish with short spines. Leaves pinnate, to 20cm long, with 5-10 pairs of leaflets (which are not necessarily opposite); each leaflet ovate, rounded yellowish- to mid-green above, paler below, usually with a secondary stipule at the base of each leaflet stalk. Flowers are borne in dense racemes, 10-20cm long, containing about 20 flowers, each pea-like, white with a yellow base to the upper petal, sweet-scented; pod hairless.
Range and habitat: Native to parts of northern America, but very widely planted in warmer parts of Europe, including southern Britain, widely naturalised further south.
Similar species: Pagoda Tree, Clammy Locust.

CLAMMY LOCUST OR STICKY LOCUST
Robinia viscosa
Height: To 12m
Characteristics: Deciduous. Closely related to, and very similar to the Locust Tree in many respects. Differs primarily in that it is stickily hairy in most parts; the leaves, petioles, and the legumes are covered with sticky hairs, readily visible to the eye or touch. The flowers are produced in late June in rather short, squat racemes, containing 15-25 rose-pink flowers.
Range and habitat: Native to southeast USA, frequently planted in southern and central Europe, including the UK as a plant of parks and gardens; less common than Locust Tree in most areas.
Similar species: Locust Tree is similar but flowers generally white, and parts not stickily hairy; Pagoda Tree has white flowers, and differs from both *Robinia* species in that the twigs are green and hairless, compared to dark and red-brown in the Locust Trees.

flower

pods

male inflorescence

habit

leaf

fruit cluster

TREE OF HEAVEN
Ailanthus altissima
Height: To 20m, occasionally more
Characteristics: Deciduous. Bark smooth grey, becoming darker and more fissured with age. Twigs smooth, brownish-red. Leaves pinnate, alternate, up to 60cm long, with 6-12 pairs of leaflets and one terminal one; leaflets ovate-lanceolate, pointed, with several large teeth towards the heart-shaped base, shiny-green above, paler below. Flowers in large, terminal panicles, with masses of small (7-8mm diameter) greenish-white flowers, strong-smelling, with flower parts in 5s. Fruits as groups of 'keys', 3-4cm long, single-seeded, brown when ripe.
Range and habitat: Native of China; widely planted as a street tree.

122

SUMAC OR STAGS HORN
Rhus typhina
Height: To 10m
Characteristics: Deciduous. A small tree or shrub, often spreading widely, and suckering freely at the base. Young twigs thick, densely hairy. Leaves pinnate, borne alternately, with 3-10 pairs of opposite leaflets and one terminal one; individual leaflets up to 10cm long, dark green, markedly toothed around the margins, unstalked. Flowers produced in very dense terminal panicles, up to 20cm long, reddish, female ones covered with down, individual flowers very small. Fruit is a collection of drupes, covered with red hairs.
Range and habitat: Native to eastern USA, widely and frequently planted for ornamental use in parks and gardens throughout Europe, naturalising readily in warmer areas.
Similar species: Common Sumac, *R. coriaria*, (not illustrated) is similar but semi-evergreen, hispid rather than downy, and with rachis (the stalk bearing the leaf-pinnae) winged at the tip.

leaf and fruiting head

FIELD MAPLE
Acer campestre
Height: To 25m, usually less
Characteristics: Deciduous. A small tree, though also occurring as a shrub, and not infrequently in hedges. Trunk sinuous, bark pale greyish-brown, fissured. Twigs brown, finely hairy, often corky and winged. Leaves symmetrically 3-5 lobed, 6-10cm long, palmate, with the 2 basal lobes usually small compared to the other 3; pink coloured when emerging, dark green above and paler below on maturity, with tufts of hairs in vein axils, yellow in autumn. Flowers in small spikes, erect, yellowish-green, male and female flowers together, produced in May; individual flowers 5-6mm diameter. Fruit with horizontal spreading wings, usually hairy, 5-6cm across.

Range and habitat: Common and widespread through most of Europe including UK; often on clay or calcareous soils. **Similar species:** Montpelier Maple.

flowering twig

habit

fruit

MONTPELIER MAPLE
Acer monspessulanum
Height: To 12m
Characteristics: Deciduous. Small tree or shrub, with broadly domed crown. Bark is greyish black, finely fissured and cracked. Leaves 3-lobed, rather similar to Field Maple, but with more triangular, wide-spreading lobes, 4-8cm long, dark green and shiny above but paler and greyish below, leathery, with tufts of hair in the vein axils; petiole orange-red, 4cm long. Flowers appear when the leaves are out, in small clusters, becoming pendent when fully out, greenish-yellow, individual flowers small (4-5mm diameter), with long slender pedicels. Fruits c. 1cm long, with two wings held parallel or overlapping, hairless.
Range and habitat: Common native in southern Europe to mid-France (not in UK), planted occasionally in parks and gardens.
Similar species: Field Maple, but inflorescence structure, and shape of fruit quite different.

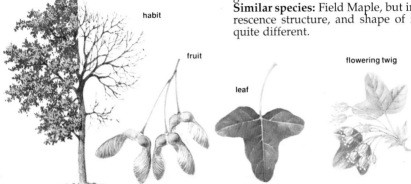

habit

fruit

leaf

flowering twig

ASH-LEAVED MAPLE OR BOX-ELDER
Acer negundo
Height: To 20m
Characteristics: Deciduous. A small, tree. Bark greyish. Leaves pinnate, (unusual amongst the maples), 5-15cm long, with 1-3 pairs of ovate leaflets and a single terminal one, not always clearly separated; leaflets shallowly toothed. Flowers on separate male and female trees: males in small clusters of greenish flowers with red anthers; females in loose pendent clusters with long peduncles; fruit has wings held almost parallel, with outer margins curving together at tips.
Range and habitat: Native of N. America; often planted for ornament.
Similar species: None.

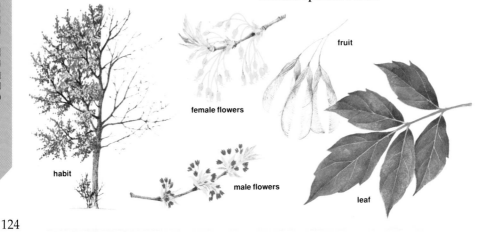

fruit

female flowers

habit

male flowers

leaf

ITALIAN MAPLE
Acer opalus
Height: To 15m, occasionally more
Characteristics: Deciduous. A small tree or spreading shrub, with a broad crown and rather twisted, low branches. Bark pinkish-orange, flaking and peeling to reveal orange patches in younger trees. Leaves palmately 3-5-lobed, lobes broad and short, dark green above paler below, hairy at first below but later with hairs along veins only; petiole red above, green below. Flowers in pendent clusters of few flowers, yellowish with slender yellow pedicels, appearing just before the leaves emerge. Fruit 2-3cm long, in clusters, with wings of individual pairs diverging at about 60 degrees, green and pink in colour.
Range and habitat: Native of mountains in southern Europe; planted rarely in parks and gardens in Britain.
Similar species: Field Maple and Montpelier Maple are most similar.

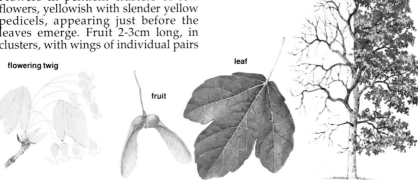

flowering twig

fruit

leaf

habit

125

flowering twig

leaf and fruit cv.'Atropurpureum'

JAPANESE MAPLE OR SMOOTH JAPANESE MAPLE
Acer palmatum

Height: To 15m

Characteristics: Deciduous. A small tall-domed tree, bushy, with a short sinuous trunk. Bark dark brown with paler markings, smooth in young trees, becoming less mottled and more fissured with age. Leaves palmately lobed, up to 10cm long, usually with 5-7 lobes, occasionally more, deeply cut more than halfway to midrib, with sharp forward-pointing teeth on margins; pale to mid-green, but often grown as one of various coloured-leaved cultivars. Flowers in upright clusters, in April-May, reddish-purple, individually 6-8mm diameter, 12-15 in a cluster, on long slender pedicels. Fruit usually pendulous, in clusters, each pair 2cm across, with widely-diverging lobes, green then reddish.

Range and habitat: Native to Japan; widely planted in parks and gardens, especially forms with strongly-coloured leaves.

Similar species: Downy Japanese Maple.

DOWNY JAPANESE MAPLE
Acer japonicum
Height: To 14m, usually less
Characteristics: Deciduous. Rather similar to Smooth Japanese Maple, and often confused with it. Occurs in several forms in cultivation. Differs from Smooth Japanese Maple in that most parts of the tree are noticeably hairy when they emerge, becoming sparsely hairy or glabrous later. Leaves are palmate, 9-13cm long, usually broader than long, with 7-11 sharply-pointed lobes that are divided to less than half-way to the base of the leaf; petiole 3-5cm long. Flowers purple, similar to Smooth Japanese Maple, appearing before the leaves in long-stalked clusters, in April-May. Fruit similar, lobes slightly more wide-spreading, on reddish pedicels.

Range and habitat: Native to Japan; planted frequently in parks and gardens, especially in forms with good autumn colours.

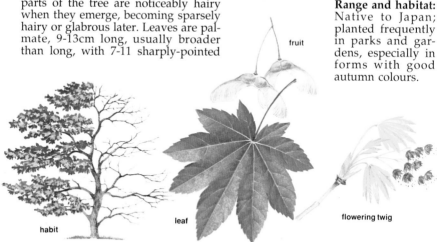

fruit

leaf

flowering twig

habit

126

leaf

habit

flowering twig

young fruit

NORWAY MAPLE
Acer platanoides
Height: To 35m
Characteristics: A tall tree, often becoming very broad with a spreading, domed crown. Leaves palmate, 5-7 lobed, shallowly divided, markedly pointed, 10-15cm long, and about as broad. The flowers are in upright clusters of 30-40, bright yellow-green, appearing before leaves in March-April, persisting until after the leaves are open. Occurs in many varietal forms, often with strongly-coloured foliage.
Range and habitat: Native to most of Europe; in Britain it is cultivated in parks and gardens.
Similar species: Sharply-pointed leaves and upright flowers distinguish it from Sycamore.

leaf

fruit

habit

flowering twig

fruit

female flowers

SYCAMORE
Acer pseudoplatanus

Height: To 35m

Characteristics: A large, domed tree, often widely-spreading. Bark greyish-brown (often green with algae), flaking in rectangles. Leaves large, as broad as long, to 15cm, 5-lobed, cut about half-way to the base; petioles pink, green or red. Flowers in long cylindrical spikes, to 12cm long, pendulous, greenish-yellow, appearing with the leaves in April-May. Fruits large, 6cm across a pair, which diverge from each other at right-angles or slightly wider; Green with a little red at first, becoming brown when ripe.

Range and habitat: Originally native to south-east Europe, now very widely planted and thoroughly naturalised throughout UK and most of Europe.

Similar species: Red Maple, *Acer rubrum*, is similar to Sycamore. The leaves are similar, with smaller basal lobes; the flowers are reddish in small clusters, appearing before the leaves. Fruit bright red, with wings diverging at a narrow angle. Native to N. America, widely planted for ornament.

habit

128

fruit and seed

leaf

flower

HORSE CHESTNUT
Aesculus hippocastanum
Height: To 25m
Characteristics: Deciduous. A familiar tree, especially for its 'conkers'. A stout, wide-spreading, large-domed tree with dense foliage. Bark dark greyish-brown, smooth when young but becoming flaky. Buds conspicuously large (up to 3cm long), deep brown, and very resinous and sticky. Leaves palmate with 5-7 leaflets cut right to the base, each leaflet obovate with a long wedge-shaped base, dark green above, paler and somewhat downy below; margins doubly-toothed, petiole long (up to 20cm). Flowers produced in conspicuous, erect, cylindrical-triangular inflorescences, up to 30cm long, with masses of flowers each white blotched with pink or yellow at base of petals. Fruit globose, green, spiny, up to 6cm diameter, containing 1-3 conkers.
Range and habitat: Native to southeast Europe, but now widely planted and naturalised.
Similar species: Red Horse Chestnut.

flower

fruit

RED HORSE CHESTNUT
Aesculus x *carnea*
Characteristics: Similar to Horse Chestnut, but smaller in all respects, and with red or pink flowers in open spikes. Fruit spineless. Hybrid between the above and a N. American species, *A. pavia*, now commonly planted.

129

COMMON HOLLY
Ilex aquifolium
Height: To 12m, occasionally much higher
Characteristics: Evergreen. A shrub or small tree, irregularly conical. Bark smooth, silvery-grey, becoming less smooth. Young twigs bright green, becoming shiny. Leaves very familiar: ovate, usually very spiny (though often unspiny high in older trees), dark green above, paler below. Male and female trees separate. Male flowers 6-8mm diameter, greenish-white, with large anthers and aborted ovary; female flowers similar, with large ovary, small anthers. Berries scarlet.
Range and habitat: Very common and widespread.

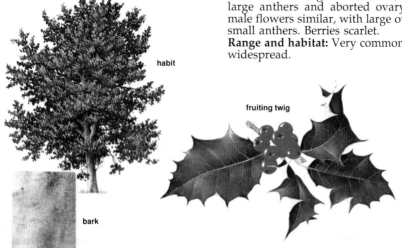

habit

bark

fruiting twig

HIGHCLERE HOLLY
Ilex x altaclarensis
Height: To 20m, usually less
Characteristics: Evergreen. Generally rather similar to Common Holly, and often confused with it, arising as a hybrid between it and Canary Holly, *Ilex perado*. The leaves are similar in colour, but with fewer, forward-pointing spines, or none at all. Flowers similar but slightly larger (to 1.2cm diameter). Fruit similar, though more ovoid, slightly larger.
Range and habitat: Of garden origin only, widely planted for ornament and shelter, especially in coastal areas and in areas of high pollution.
Similar species: Common Holly.

habit

fruiting twig

flowering twig

COMMON SPINDLE TREE
Euonymus europaeus
Height: To 6m
Characteristics: A shrub or very small tree. Bark smooth and grey, more fissured and pinker with age. Twigs green, 4-angled when young. Leaves ovate-lanceolate, to 10cm long, pointed, sharply-toothed. Inflorescence is a branched cluster of pale green flowers (illustration gives the impression of flowers being too white), 8-10mm diameter, with 4 petals. Fruits attractive, with bright pink, 4-part capsule splitting to reveal orange berries.
Range and habitat: Common through UK and most of Europe, especially on lime-rich soils.
Similar species: Broad-leaved Spindle Tree.

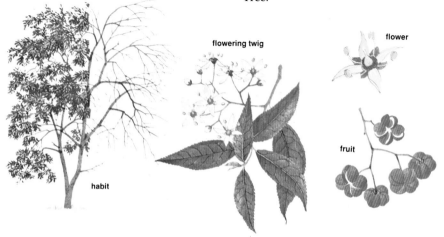

flowering twig

flower

fruit

habit

BROAD-LEAVED SPINDLE TREE
Euonymus latifolius
Height: To 7m
Characteristics: Deciduous. Generally rather similar to, and closely-related to, Common Spindle. The main differences are that the young twigs are not distinctly 4-angled; the buds are very long and slender (7-12mm long, compared to 2-4mm in Common Spindle). The leaves are larger (up to 16cm long), broader and more rounded, without the pointed tip, with margins untoothed or finely toothed. The inflorescence has between 4 and 12 flowers, each of which has 5 petals (not 4), which are slightly greenish-pink, rounded at the tips. The flowers are produced in May-June.The capsule is similar in colour, but with 5 lobes and much more sharply angled.
Range and habitat: Native to southern and central Europe, where it is common in woods and scrub. Occasionally planted for ornament in UK.
Similar species: Common Spindle.

flowering twig

flower

fruit

131

JAPANESE SPINDLE TREE
Euonymus japonicus
Height: To 6m
Characteristics: Evergreen. Unlikely to be confused with the 2 European *Euonymus* species, from which it differs considerably. Occurs as an erect, small tree or shrub, and often as a hedging plant. Twigs grey, slightly 4-angled. Leaves thick and rather leathery, roughly ovate, pointed or blunt, with finely-toothed margins, dark green above and rather paler green below. Flowers greenish-yellow, small, with parts in 4s, produced in long open axillary clusters, though they are rarely prolific or conspicuous. Flowering period June-July. Capsules are small, (to 8mm wide), rounded, pinkish in colour – not a significant feature as in the European species.
Range and habitat: Native to Japan, and east Asia, but widely planted in Europe, in seaside areas especially, for ornament, cover, and shelter. Occasionally naturalised in warmer areas.
Similar species: None.

flower

flowering twig

fruit

132

female flower

flowering twig

male flower

habit

BOX
Buxus sempervirens

Height: To 5m, occasionally more
Characteristics: Evergreen. A shrub or very small tree, often with several stems from the base, frequently leaning to one side. Bark pale-brown, becoming corky and fissured with age. Twigs 4-angled, green and hairy when young. Leaves in opposite pairs, small (1.5-3cm long), ovate-elliptical, usually with a notch at the tip, dark glossy green above, paler green below, hairy at the end nearest the stem; margin untoothed, rolled under, petiole very short, orange, and hairy. Flowers are greenish-yellow, very small individually (3-5mm diameter), in dense axillary clusters, male and females together, produced in April. The fruit is a globose-ovate capsule, with 3 horns (developed from the styles), up to 1cm long, green becoming grey or brown, with black shiny seeds.
Range and habitat: Widespread in most of southern Europe, rare in UK as a native, though often planted. Usually on lime-rich soils.
Similar species: None.

FLOWERING MAPLE
Corynabutilon vitifolium
Height: To 8m
Characteristics: Deciduous. Not related to the maples, though the leaves look rather similar – actually a member of the mallow family. Young shoots downy. Leaves alternate, triangular, with 3-5 triangular lobes, cut about a third of the way to the midrib; margin coarsely toothed. Flowers conspicuous in a cyme of 1-5 large flowers 5-7cm diameter, pale bluish-pink in colour, with rounded overlapping petals. Fruit splits into several segments when ripe.
Range and habitat: Native to coastal Chile; planted in milder coastal areas.
Similar species: None, if combination of flowers and leaves is available.

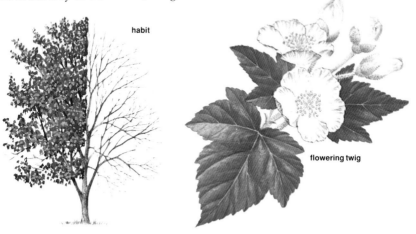

habit

flowering twig

133

BUCKTHORN
Rhamnus catharticus
Height: To 6m, occasionally to 10m
Characteristics: Deciduous. A shrub or very small tree. Bark grey, becoming nearly black in older trees, scaling off to reveal orangey patches. Twigs may bear spines, scattered through the bush. Leaves ovate, more or less opposite, 3-7cm long, with 2-4 pairs of distinct lateral veins, apex blunt, pointed or notched; margins finely toothed. Male and female flowers on separate plants; both small, 3-4mm diameter, greenish, in clusters or solitary, with 4 (or occasionally 5) parts. Fruits are black when ripe, roughly spherical, 6-8mm in diameter.
Range and habitat: Throughout most of Europe except far south and north; common in England on calcareous soils, in scrub and woodland edges.
Similar species: Alder Buckthorn is somewhat similar.

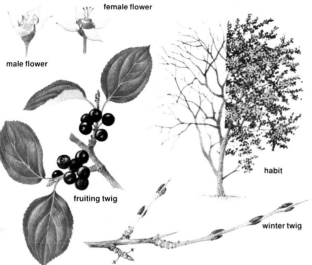

female flower

male flower

fruiting twig

habit

winter twig

ALDER BUCKTHORN
Frangula alnus
Height: To 5m
Characteristics: Deciduous. A shrub or very small tree. Closely related to Buckthorn, though readily distinguished by the detailed differences. Alder Buckthorn is spineless, young twigs green at first, becoming brown later. Leaves roughly ovate, widest above the middle, 4-7cm long, bluntly pointed, untoothed, shiny mid-green above, paler below and hairy when young, with 7-9 pairs of not very conspicuous lateral veins; petiole reddish, short. Flowers small, about 3mm in diameter, in clusters or solitary, with male and female parts in one 5-part flower, in May-June. Fruits spherical-ovoid, to 1cm, yellow, red, then black.
Range and habitat: Common and widespread through most of Europe, including the UK. Usual habitat is damp woodland and fens.
Similar species: Buckthorn.

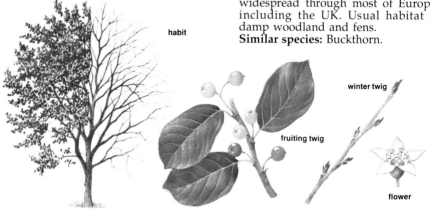

habit

winter twig

fruiting twig

flower

134

SILVER LIME
Tilia tomentosa (including Weeping Silver Lime, *T. petiolaris*)
Height: To 30m
Characteristics: Deciduous. Bark greenish-grey, ridged and fissured. Young twigs tomentose. Leaves suborbicular, with tapering tip, and uneven heart-shaped base, dark green and smooth above, but distinctly silvery-white, hairy below; margin sharply toothed, petiole to 5cm, densely pubescent. Flower bracts lanceolate, pubescent. Flowers whitish in pendent clusters of 5-10 on long peduncles. Fruit ovoid, to 1cm long, downy.
Range and habitat: Native to southeast Europe; widely planted.
Similar species: *T. petiolaris* is similar but weeping.

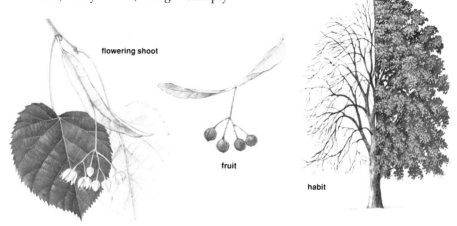

flowering shoot

fruit

habit

SMALL-LEAVED LIME
Tilia cordata
Height: To 30m
Characteristics: Deciduous. A tall, slender tree, with an irregularly-domed shape and a dense crown. Bark grey and smooth when young. Branches arched and drooping on old open-grown trees. Leaves generally smaller than those of Large-leaved Lime (though individual ones may not be), often almost circular, with short point and heart-shaped base; rather greyish below, with tufts of rusty-coloured hairs in the axils of the veins; margin finely-toothed. Bracts pale green, lanceolate. Flowers very pale, in clusters of 5-15 held obliquely upright, June-July. Fruit ovoid to globose, small (5-6mm), slightly ribbed, usually hairless at maturity.
Range and habitat: Widespread as native tree in most of Europe; in UK an uncommon old woodland species, though also planted for ornament.
Similar species: Large-leaved Lime has larger leaves, pendent flowers, and no rusty hairs under the leaves. Common Lime.

135

flowering shoot

fruit

habit

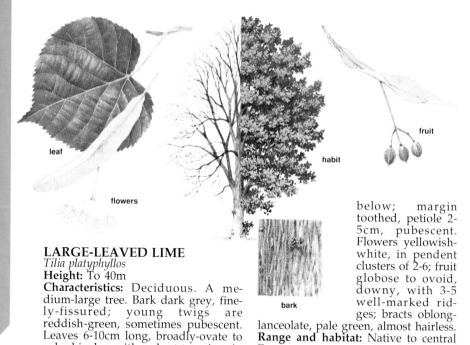

leaf

flowers

habit

fruit

bark

136

LARGE-LEAVED LIME
Tilia platyphyllos
Height: To 40m
Characteristics: Deciduous. A medium-large tree. Bark dark grey, finely-fissured; young twigs are reddish-green, sometimes pubescent. Leaves 6-10cm long, broadly-ovate to suborbicular, with a short tapering tip and heart-shaped base, dark green above, paler, usually softly hairy below; margin toothed, petiole 2-5cm, pubescent. Flowers yellowish-white, in pendent clusters of 2-6; fruit globose to ovoid, downy, with 3-5 well-marked ridges; bracts oblong-lanceolate, pale green, almost hairless.
Range and habitat: Native to central Europe; rare as a native in parts of southern UK, also widely planted.
Similar species: Other limes.

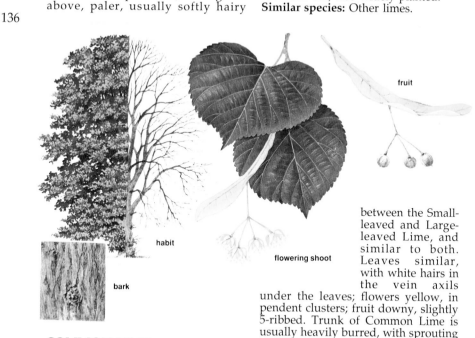

habit

bark

flowering shoot

fruit

COMMON LIME
Tilia x vulgaris
Height: To 45m
Characteristics: Originated as a hybrid between the Small-leaved and Large-leaved Lime, and similar to both. Leaves similar, with white hairs in the vein axils under the leaves; flowers yellow, in pendent clusters; fruit downy, slightly 5-ribbed. Trunk of Common Lime is usually heavily burred, with sprouting small branches, whereas the two species limes are clean-boled.
Range and habitat: Very widely planted in streets, parks and gardens.

CAUCASIAN LIME
Tilia x *euchlora*
Height: To 20m.
Characteristics: Deciduous. A hybrid between Small-leaved Lime and a west

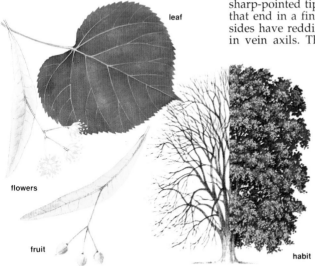

leaf

flowers

fruit

habit

Asian species, *T. dasystyla*, sharing the characteristics of both, and easily confused with other limes. Main characteristics are: clean trunk without burrs; bright green, usually shiny, hairless twigs; leaves narrow abruptly to a sharp-pointed tip, with marginal teeth that end in a fine hair-like tip; undersides have reddish tufts of hair below in vein axils. The flowers are a rich buttery yellow, occurring in pendent clusters of 3-7. Fruit tapered at both ends, ovoid, 1-1.3cm long, slightly 5-ribbed, downy.
Range and habitat: Frequently planted in Europe as a street tree, including the UK, where it is local.
Similar species: Small-leaved, Common and Large-leaved Limes.

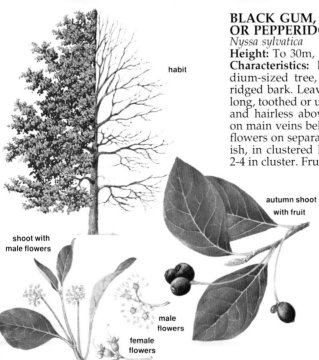

habit

shoot with male flowers

male flowers

female flowers

autumn shoot with fruit

BLACK GUM, TUPELO OR PEPPERIDGE
Nyssa sylvatica
Height: To 30m, 15m in cultivation
Characteristics: Deciduous. A medium-sized tree, with brownish-grey ridged bark. Leaves ovate, up to 15cm long, toothed or untoothed, dark green and hairless above, paler and downy on main veins below. Male and female flowers on separate trees; males greenish, in clustered heads; females small, 2-4 in cluster. Fruits ovoid, 1-2cm long, fleshy, bluish-black in small clusters.
Range and habitat: Native of eastern USA. Planted ornamentally for its striking scarlet and gold autumn foliage; not common in UK gardens.
Similar species: None.

HANDKERCHIEF TREE, DOVE TREE OR GHOST TREE

Davidia involucrata
Height: To 20m
Characteristics: Deciduous. Bark greyish-brown, finely flaking and fissuring. Leaves broadly ovate, up to 15cm long, heart-shaped at the base, pointed at the tip, pale and pubescent below; margins with triangular pointed teeth, petiole long (to 15cm), green, or often pink or red. Flowers small in dense heads, mainly male, with purplish stamens; more conspicuous is the pair of large asymmetrical white bracts up to 16cm long and 10cm wide below the flowers. Fruit ovoid, deep green ripening purplish.
Range and habitat: Native of China; widely planted for ornament.

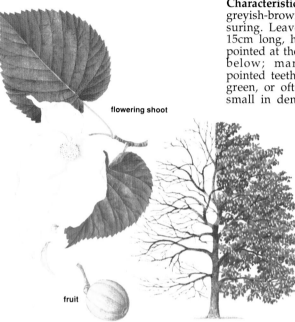

flowering shoot

fruit

habit

138

NYMANS' HYBRID EUCRYPHIA AND OTHER EUCRYPHIA SPECIES

Eucryphia x *nymansensis* 'Nymansay'
Height: To 15m

Characteristics: Evergreen. A group of shrubs or small trees grown for their attractive late summer flowers; they originate from Chile and Australia, but those grown in gardens are mainly of garden origin, especially Nymans' hybrid, the result of a cross between *E. glutinosa* and *E. cordifolia*. Leaves variable, simple ovate when young, trifoliate when mature; margins toothed, glossy green above, paler below and pubescent on the veins. Flowers produced from late August to mid-September, mainly on upper parts of the tree; large, 6-8cm diameter, white, with 4 or 5 petals, and a mass of pinkish stamens.
Range and habitat: *Eucryphia* x *nymansensis* and *E.* x *intermedia* are both frequent in parks and larger gardens in the UK, especially in the west.
Similar species: None.

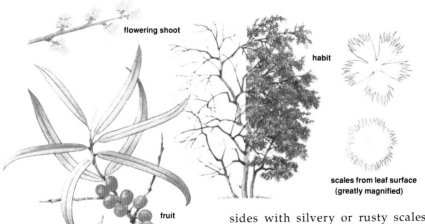

flowering shoot

habit

scales from leaf surface
(greatly magnified)

fruit

SEA BUCKTHORN
Hippophae rhamnoides
Height: To 10m, usually much less
Characteristics: Deciduous. A much-branched, dense, spreading shrub. Young twigs covered with silvery scales, spiny. Leaves simple, linear, untoothed, alternate, and covered on both sides with silvery or rusty scales; densely crowded on shoots. Flowers small and inconspicuous, appearing before the leaves, with separate male and female plants; individual flowers greenish, about 3mm diameter. Fruits much more conspicuous, bright orange ovoid-spherical berries, 6-8mm diameter, in clusters.
Range and habitat: Coastal areas, and occasionally mountains, throughout UK and Europe.

139

OLEASTER
Elaeagnus angustifolia
Height: To 12m
Characteristics: Deciduous. A shrub or small tree, occasionally spiny. The young twigs are covered with shiny silvery scales, becoming darker as they mature. Leaves linear-lanceolate, sometimes slightly broader, matt green above, paler and covered with silvery scales on the underside. Flowers yellow inside, silvery outside, tubular, about 1cm long, fragrant, in small groups in the leaf axils, appearing before or with the leaves in May-June. Fruit ovoid, 1-2cm long, greenish when young (sometimes confused with olives), becoming orange, succulent.
Range and habitat: A native of Western Asia, widely planted in southern and central Europe for ornament and hedging; also widely naturalised.
Similar species: Silverberry is similar, with brown young twigs and dry fruit.

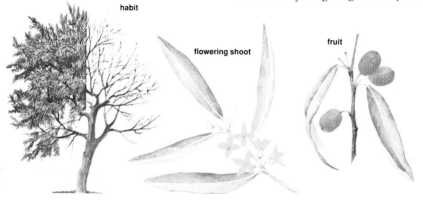

habit

flowering shoot

fruit

FRENCH TAMARISK
Tamarix gallica
Height: To 8m
Characteristics: Deciduous. A shrub or small bushy tree; very feathery in appearance. Bark purplish-brown. Leaves short and scale-like, about 1-2mm long, ovate in shape, pressed against the stems. Flowers in racemes, 2-3cm long, in April-May; individual flowers are very small, about 4mm across, with 5 tiny pink petals which fall soon after the flower opens; the filaments of the stamens are not swollen at the base (whereas they are in some other species of tamarisk).
Range and habitat: Native to southern Europe and most of France as a coastal species; also widely planted for shelter, ornament and stabilisation.
Similar species: Other tamarisks, not native to the area.

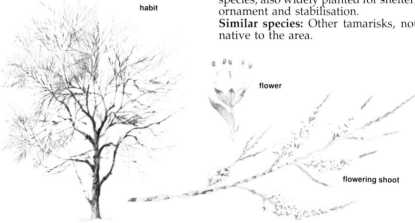

habit

flower

flowering shoot

140

LEMON-SCENTED SPOTTED GUM
Eucalyptus citriodora
Height: To 40m, though usually less
Characteristics: Evergreen. A tall, slender tree, with smooth pale greyish bark. Leaves of *Eucalyptus* occur in two forms: juvenile and adult (and sometimes a third, intermediate) which are often quite different. Juvenile leaves are oblong to ovate, rough and bristly, opposite then alternate; adult leaves lanceolate, to 25cm by 1-4cm, strongly lemon-scented, mid-green. Inflorescence is a branched, flattened spike in the leaf axils, with 3-5 flowers; anthers white. Fruits globose or elongated, strongly contracted at the mouth.
Range and habitat: Native to Australia, but grown for ornament in southern Europe.
Similar species: Lemon-scented leaves distinctive.

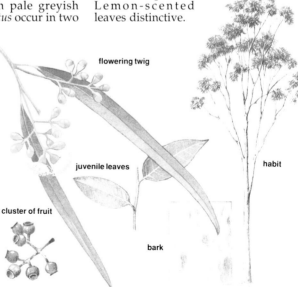

flowering twig

juvenile leaves

cluster of fruit

bark

habit

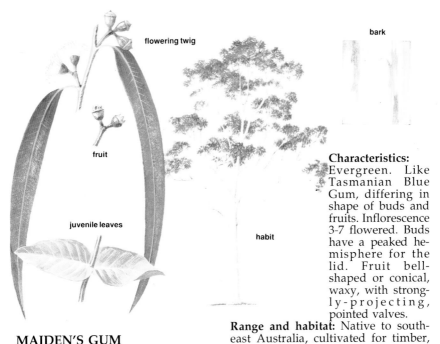

flowering twig

bark

fruit

juvenile leaves

habit

Characteristics:
Evergreen. Like Tasmanian Blue Gum, differing in shape of buds and fruits. Inflorescence 3-7 flowered. Buds have a peaked hemisphere for the lid. Fruit bell-shaped or conical, waxy, with strong-ly-projecting, pointed valves.
Range and habitat: Native to south-east Australia, cultivated for timber, etc. in southern Europe, and occasionally for ornament further north.

MAIDEN'S GUM
Eucalyptus maidenii
Height: To 40m, usually less

141

TASMANIAN BLUE GUM
Eucalyptus globulus
Height: To 50m, more in native habitat
Characteristics: Evergreen. A medium irregularly-shaped tree. Bark smooth, blue-grey. Juvenile foliage blue-green, ovate or broadly lanceolate, to 15cm long, in opposite pairs at first, heart-shaped at the base or clasping the stem. Adult leaves lanceolate, to 30cm long, sickle-shaped, leathery, dark green, borne alternately, with a short petiole. Inflorescence consists of 1-3 flowers, axillary; buds up to 3cm, glaucous, with a thick warty disc-shaped 'lid'; anthers yellow. Fruit top-shaped or flattened spherical, to 2cm, 4-angled, warty, ribbed, with a large thick disc at the end.
Range and habitat: Native to Australia, but widely planted in southern Europe, and occasionally further north.

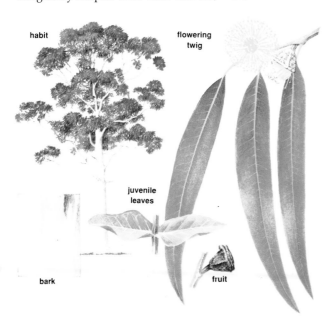

habit

flowering twig

juvenile leaves

bark

fruit

CIDER GUM
Eucalyptus gunnii
Height: To 30m
Characteristics: Evergreen. A medium-sized tree. Bark smooth. Juvenile leaves ovate to round, heart-shaped at base, sessile, often grey-green, in opposite pairs. Adult leaves variably lanceolate, to 7cm, mid-green. Inflorescence is a 3-flowered umbel, whitish-yellow; buds club-shaped, with a red peaked 'lid', much shorter than the calyx tube. Fruit bell-shaped or almost hemispherical, with a small depressed disc at the end, and 3-5 narrow slightly-projecting valves.
Range and habitat: Cultivated in southern England.

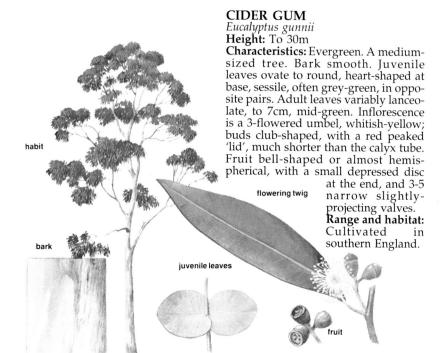

habit

flowering twig

bark

juvenile leaves

fruit

142

POMEGRANATE
Punica granatum
Height: To 8m, usually less
Characteristics: Deciduous. A shrub or very small tree. Leaves in opposite pairs, lanceolate to obovate, to 8cm long, untoothed, on a short petiole. Flowers solitary or paired, hermaphrodite, terminal, large (up to 4cm in diameter), red (or occasionally white) with thick, leathery, reddish sepals; flowers in midsummer to autumn. Fruit familiar: globose, to 10cm diameter, red to yellowish, with numerous fleshy seeds.
Range and habitat: Native to southwest Asia; widely cultivated in southern Europe, occasionally further north.

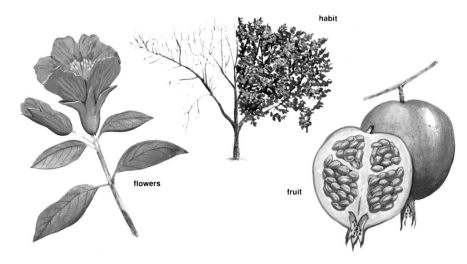

habit

flowers

fruit

CORNELIAN CHERRY
Cornus mas

Height: To 10m, usually less
Characteristics: Deciduous shrub. Twigs greenish-yellow. Leaves opposite, ovate to elliptic, up to 10cm long, untoothed. Flowers in small clusters, yellow with greenish bracts that soon fall, before the leaves open, in February-March. Fruit is a berry, 1-2cm long, bright red when ripe.
Range and habitat: Native to parts of southern-central Europe, naturalised and planted elsewhere including UK.

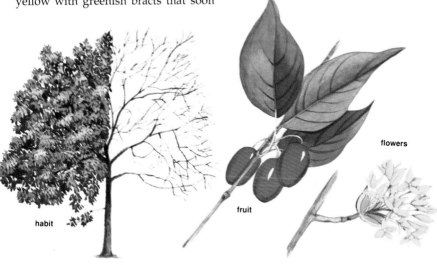

flowers

fruit

habit

DOGWOOD
Cornus sanguinea (Thelycrania sanguinea)

Height: To 4m
Characteristics: Deciduous. A shrub, with dark red distinctive twigs, which are very conspicuous when leafless in winter. Leaves opposite, oval to elliptic, pointed, untoothed, with 3-4 pairs of distinct veins; reddish-green above, paler and hairy below. Become strong red colour in autumn. Flowers in terminal clusters, quite showy *en masse*, though individually small (to 1cm), greenish-white, produced in June-July. Fruit usually globose or ovoid, 5-8mm, becoming black when fully ripe.
Range and habitat: A widespread native throughout most of Europe except the extreme north and south. Common in south UK, mainly on calcareous soils. Occurs on downs, woodland edges, scrub, and hedgerows, occasionally dominant on chalk.
Similar species: No similar native species.

flowers

fruit

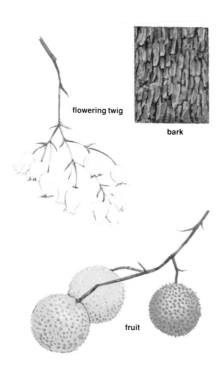

flowering twig

bark

fruit

STRAWBERRY TREE
Arbutus unedo
Height: To 9m
Characteristics: Evergreen. A shrub or small tree, with a short bole and dense rounded crown. The bark is distinctive, red with peeling and shredding brownish strips. Young twigs pinkish or red, hairy. Leaves ovate-lanceolate, up to 12cm long, dark glossy green above but paler below, hairy at the base, and with a prominent midrib; margin untoothed or toothed sharply, petiole hairy, to 1cm long. Flowers appear in a drooping panicle, with individual flowers bell-shaped, white, produced in autumn at the same time as the ripening fruits from the previous year. The fruit is a globose berry, to 2cm diameter, covered with conical bumps, ripening reddish. A member of the heather family.
Range and habitat: A Mediterranean species, found in warm dry rocky areas, but also native to south-west Eire. Widely planted elsewhere, naturalising readily in warmer conditions.
Similar species: Eastern Strawberry Tree.

EASTERN STRAWBERRY TREE
Arbutus andrachne
Height: To 12m
Characteristics: Evergreen. The eastern Mediterranean equivalent of the Strawberry Tree. It differs in that the bark is paler, the young twigs are hairless and yellowish-green. The flowers occur in erect (not pendent) panicles, which are produced in spring (not autumn). The fruit is a smaller (roughly 1cm diameter) spherical berry, smoother, without warts.
Range and habitat: Native to the eastern Mediterranean area. Occasionally planted elsewhere. A hybrid with Common Strawberry Tree occurs in the wild and in cultivation.

fruit

habit

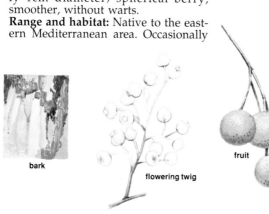

bark

flowering twig

STORAX
Styrax officinale
Height: To 7m, but usually less
Characteristics: Deciduous. A shrub or small tree, with a rounded crown and smooth grey bark. All parts of the shrub have branched hairs. Leaves are ovate to almost oblong, 3-7cm long, borne alternately, rather blunt at the tip, rounded at the base, mid-green above, paler below, hairy on both surfaces, though noticeably hairier underneath; margin untoothed, petiole about 1cm, hairy. The flowers occur in loose drooping racemes, each containing between 3 and 6 bell-shaped, deeply cut whitish flowers, about 2cm in diameter, produced in April-May; the flower stalks are 1-2cm long, densely hairy. The fruits are ovoid, to 2cm long, greyish and hairy, tipped with the remains of the style. The aromatic gum, storax, comes from the sap of this species.
Range and habitat: Native to the eastern Mediterranean, but cultivated and naturalised elsewhere in southern Europe.
Similar species: Snowbell Tree.

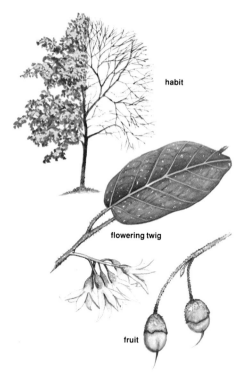

habit

flowering twig

fruit

SNOWBELL TREE
Styrax japonica
Height: To 11m
Characteristics: Deciduous. A shrub or small tree, with a rounded dense crown. Bark greyish, striped with pink when young, becoming darker with age. Leaves roughly ovate, long-pointed, 6-8cm long, borne alternately, wedge-shaped at the base, shiny green above, paler below; margin wavy, barely toothed, petiole very short, yellowish. Flowers produced abundantly in the form of hanging clusters, each containing 2-4 flowers on slender stalks 2-4cm long; individual flowers similar to Storax, very attractive white and bell-shaped, with 4 or 5 petals. Flowers in June and July. Fruit globose, up to 1.5cm long, greenish-grey, attached to the persistent starry-lobed calyx.
Range and habitat: Native to China and Japan, now frequently grown as an ornamental in parks and gardens in the UK and elsewhere.
Similar species: Storax has different fruit, different leaf shape, and flowers earlier.

FLOWERING ASH
OR MANNA ASH
Fraxinus ornus
Height: To 25m
Characteristics: Deciduous. A close relative of Common Ash, with rather similar leaves, but with much more showy bunches of creamy-white, fragrant flowers (hence the name 'Flowering Ash') in May. Fruits typical of ashes, i.e. bunches of slender samara (or keys) turning brown as they ripen.
Range and habitat: Native to Europe as far north as north France, and widely planted for ornament further north.

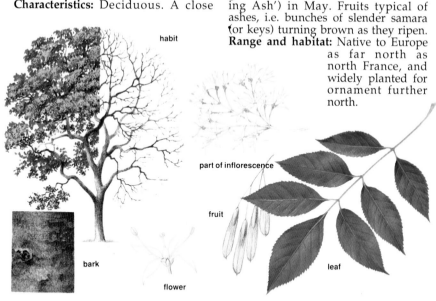

habit

part of inflorescence

fruit

leaf

bark

flower

146

NARROW-LEAVED ASH
Fraxinus angustifolia
Height: To 25m
Characteristics: Very similar to Common Ash. The main differences are: the buds are brown, downy, rather than greenish-black; the leaflets are distinctly narrower than those of Common Ash, and more toothed, with a long pointed tip; the flowers appear in March-April, maturing into similar-looking keys, with a less marked apical spine than those of Common Ash.
Range and habitat: Native to southern Europe, but also infrequently planted in parks and gardens further north, including in the UK.

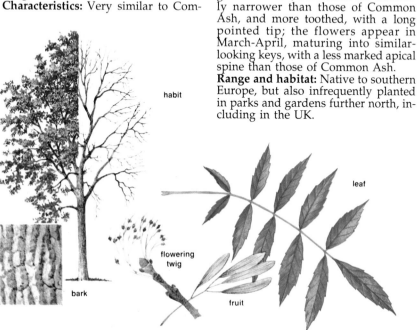

habit

leaf

flowering twig

bark

fruit

habit

flowering twig

male flower

leaf

fruit

COMMON ASH
Fraxinus excelsior

Height: To 40m

Characteristics: Deciduous. A familiar and well-loved tree. Bark pale grey, smooth when young, becoming strongly fissured on older trees. Twigs flattened at the nodes, buds conical and slightly greenish-black. Leaves pinnate, up to 35cm long, with 3-6 opposite pairs of leaflets and a terminal one; leaflets ovate-lanceolate, toothed, pointed, dark green above, paler below with white hairs around the midrib. Flowers produced in small axillary panicles, appearing before the leaves in March-May; individual flowers very small, purple. Trees may have all male flowers, all female, completely mixed, different sexes on different branches, or may even change annually. Fruit are the familiar samaras (keys) 2-4cm, with a spine at the tip, green then brown.

Range and habitat: Common throughout UK and Europe, especially on base-rich or clay soils. Frequently cultivated, including a pendulous form.

Similar species: Narrow-leaved Ash.

COMMON PRIVET
Ligustrum vulgare
Height: To 4m
Characteristics: Semi-evergreen. A small shrub, densely-branched and spreading widely when open-grown, though most often seen as an unattractive clipped hedge plant. Leaves lanceolate, (4-8cm long), thin but slightly leathery, untoothed, very short-stalked, green above and paler below. Flowers creamy-white, fragrant (though not always thought of as pleasant), in dense pyramidal panicles, produced in May-June. The fruits are globose berries, becoming shiny black when fully ripe, borne in terminal clusters; poisonous to humans.
Range and habitat: A very common and widespread species through most of south and central Europe, including England. Planted for hedging and ornament here and elsewhere, and frequently naturalising.
Similar species: Garden privet has broader leaves and hairless young shoots.

flower

fruit

148

OLIVE
Olea europaea
Height: To 15m
Characteristics: Evergreen. A small-medium tree, becoming broad and spreading with gnarled and twisted branches and trunk. Bark silvery-grey, finely fissured and cracked. Leaves opposite, lanceolate, up to 8cm long, untoothed, leathery in texture, pale and rather scaly below. Flowers borne in axillary panicles of masses of small greenish-white fragrant flowers with 4 parts. The fruit is ovoid, becoming green, brown or black when mature – the familiar olive, in its cultivated form – but fruits on wild forms are smaller.
Range and habitat: Native to southern Europe, growing in dry rocky places. Widely cultivated for the fruit.
Similar species: Phillyrea.

flower

habit

fruit

flowering twig

PHILLYREA
Phillyrea latifolia
Height: To 12m
Characteristics: Evergreen. Sometimes confused with Olive. Bark grey and smooth, becoming ridged. Leaves in opposite pairs, ovate-lanceolate in shape, to 7cm in juvenile form, narrower and more lanceolate as adult foliage; very dark glossy green above, paler and matt below, with 7-11 pairs of lateral veins clearly visible. Flowers borne in shorter axillary racemes than those of Olive; greenish-white, 4-lobed. Fruit is globose, to 1cm diameter, not fleshy, blue-black when ripe.
Range and habitat: Native of south Europe, planted in southern coastal areas in UK.

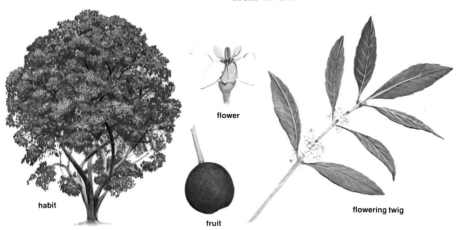

flower

habit

fruit

flowering twig

149

COMMON LILAC
Syringa vulgaris
Height: To 7m, but usually less
Characteristics: Deciduous. A familiar garden shrub or small tree, with a rounded crown, often with several branches from the base, sometimes surrounded by suckers. Bark brownish-grey, slightly stringy. Leaves opposite, undivided, ovate or somewhat heart-shaped, up to 8cm long, untoothed, hairless, dark yellowish-green above, paler below. Flowers in dense inflorescences, in May or June, usually in pairs or singly, towards the ends of shoots, up to 20cm long; individual flowers pink or white, tubular with 4 corolla lobes, fragrant. Fruit is a narrow, pointed capsule, c. 1cm long.
Range and habitat: Native to southeast Europe; very widely cultivated in parks and gardens throughout Europe.

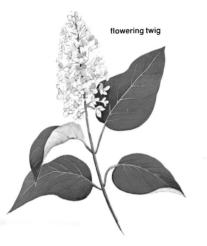

flowering twig

fruit

habit

flower

habit

fruit

leaf

flower head

INDIAN BEAN TREE
Catalpa bignonioides
Height: To 20m
Characteristics: Deciduous. A broadly-domed medium-sized tree, with a short slender trunk; bark grey-brown, smooth at first, becoming fissured. Leaves in opposite pairs, or in whorls of 3, broadly ovate or heart-shaped, up to 25cm long at most, and almost as broad, mid-green above, paler below; margin entire, or shallowly lobed, petiole long (10-18cm), flattened. Flowers conspicuous in large paniculate heads up to 25cm long, produced in midsummer; individual flowers bell-shaped with 5 spreading petal lobes, white with purple and yellow spots in the throat and on the lower lip, up to 5cm in diameter. Fruit is a bean-like capsule, pendulous, long and thin, up to 40cm – the 'bean' of the name.
Range and habitat: A native of southeast USA. (The 'Indian' in the name is the N. American Indian), widely planted for ornament in streets, parks and gardens through much of Europe except the north.

FOXGLOVE TREE
Paulownia tomentosa
Height: To 10-15m, occasionally larger
Characteristics: Deciduous. An attractive small-medium tree. Leaves opposite, roughly ovate with a heart-shaped base, partially divided into three lobes; pubescent green above, densely pubescent and greyer below; petiole very long, pubescent. Flowers in erect heads, up to 30cm high; flower buds attractively brown, pubescent, flowers large bell-shaped-tubular, violet.
Range and habitat: Native of China; widely planted in southern Europe, land in UK parks and gardens.

fruit

flower head

habit

leaf from a young tree

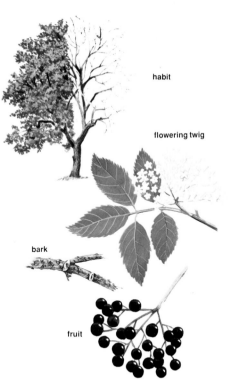

habit

flowering twig

bark

fruit

ELDER
Sambucus nigra
Height: To 10m, usually less
Characteristics: Deciduous. A small tree or shrub, branching frequently at, or close to, the base. Bark greyish-brown, deeply grooved and becoming rather corky on older trees. Basal shoots often have a white pithy centre. Leaves opposite, pinnate, with 2-4 pairs of leaflets and one terminal one, each roughly ovate, pointed, with sharp teeth, mid-green above, paler and hairier below. Flowers occur in large, conspicuous, flat-topped or slightly rounded clusters, 10-20cm in diameter, produced in June, containing numerous small creamy-white flowers, heavily scented or pungent. Fruits are globose, 5-7mm diameter, with 3-5 stone cells, becoming shiny purplish black, juicy and edible, though not good.
Range and habitat: A very widespread species in Europe, occurring on waste ground, in woods, hedges etc., generally preferring high nutrient levels.
Similar species: Alpine Elder.

151

ALPINE ELDER
OR BERRY-BEARING ELDER
Sambucus racemosa
Height: To 5m
Characteristics: Deciduous. Generally similar to Common Elder in characteristics, this species is the mountain counterpart, though the two overlap in range in places. A spreading shrub with arching branches and grey bark; pith of twigs reddish-brown (whitish in Common Elder). Leaves pinnate, with 1-3 pairs of leaflets, individually ovate, hairless, (except when young) sharply toothed, mid-green above, paler below. Flowers occur in dense pyramid-shaped panicles (not flat-topped, as in Common Elder), up to 10cm tall, with individual flowers small and creamy-yellow, produced between April and June. Fruit similar in shape to elderberries, but ripening shiny bright red, not purple-black.
Range and habitat: Primarily a mountain species, in woods and on open slopes, through most of Continental Europe; not native to UK, but introduced and naturalised particularly in Scotland.

flowering twig

fruit

GUELDER ROSE
Viburnum opulus
Height: To 4m
Characteristics: Deciduous. A spreading bushy shrub; twigs green at first, angled, becoming browner; older bark pale-brown, streaked and marked. Leaves 3- (or occasionally 5-) lobed, roughly triangular in outline, 4-10cm long, and often as broad, each lobe triangular to rectangular, pointed; dark green above, paler and hairy below; petiole 1-3cm, often green below and reddish above. Inflorescence is a plate-like, flat-topped or slightly-curved cluster, with a ring of large, sterile, white outer flowers surrounding the fertile, smaller inner flowers. Flowers in May-June. Fruit in the form of a cluster of berries, which ripen to red, 0.8-1cm in diameter.
Range and habitat: A common and widespread species of woods, scrub, hedges, etc., throughout most of Europe, especially in damp places. Also planted for ornament in various forms, especially with yellow berries.
Similar species: Leaves could be confused with a maple.

152

WAYFARING TREE
Viburnum lantana
Height: To 6m
Characteristics: Deciduous. A shrub or very small bushy tree, with brownish bark, grey hairy rounded twigs, and naked buds (i.e. without bud-scales, so that the leaves are clearly visible even in bud). Leaves roughly ovate or obovate – quite different to the closely-related Guelder Rose leaves – rough, with small marginal teeth, darker green above and paler and hairy below. The inflorescence differs from that of Guelder Rose in that all the flowers are uniform, without the outer large sterile ones; they are small, creamy-white, 5-8mm diameter, clustered in a dense rounded head, produced in May-June. The fruits are ovoid and distinctly flattened, green then red then black.
Range and habitat: Native to much of Europe, though absent as a native from further north; occurs in scrub, open woodland, rocky places, often on calcareous soils. Introduced and naturalised in northern Britain and Scandinavia.

flowering twig

fruit

LAURUSTINUS
Viburnum tinus

Height: To 7m

Characteristics: Evergreen. A dense bushy shrub or small tree. Twigs glabrous, slightly angled, often reddish. Leaves ovate to lanceolate, sometimes more rounded, wedge-shaped at the base, shiny green above, paler and hairy below; margins untoothed, petiole very short, no stipules. The inflorescence is rather similar to that of wayfaring tree – a dense terminal cluster of small, white, 5-petalled flowers, with reddish peduncles, with the flowers all uniformly fertile. The size of the inflorescence is between 4 and 9cm in diameter. Flowers produced in April. The fruits are ovoid-globose, 7-9mm long, ripening to dark blue.

Range and habitat: Native to southern Europe, where it grows in dry rocky places, woods and scrub; however, it is also very widely planted for ornamental use and shelter in parks and gardens throughout Europe. Common in the UK.

Similar species: None native in the area.

flowering twig

fruit

flower

fruit

habit

leaf

fruit

habit

CABBAGE PALM
Cordyline australis
Height: To 12m
Characteristics: Evergreen. A small tree, with very distinct trunk (or several trunks, arising from root suckers), topped by a plume of foliage and flowers. Bark pale grey-fawn coloured, ridged and cracked, obscured higher up by dead leaf bases. Leaves very long, reaching almost a metre, linear-lanceolate, tapering to a long point, with numerous more or less parallel veins; dark green, usually produced in one enormous tuft, with the majority erect, and the lowest ones drooping down the stem. Flowers produced in June-July in large terminal panicles, up to a metre or more long, consisting of masses of small (c. 1cm diameter) creamy-white flowers, with 6 parts, fragrant. Fruits are small bluish-white berries, globose, in clusters.
Range and habitat: Native to New Zealand; commonly planted in south and west Europe for ornament. In UK confined to the south and west coasts.
Similar species: None widely cultivated.

EUROPEAN FAN PALM
Chamaerops humilis
Height: To 3m
Characteristics: A short-stemmed or stemless shrub or tree. In the wild, it often occurs as a very small plant, with a cluster of leaves on a tiny trunk, but in cultivation, in favourable circumstances, it can develop into a small tree. Bole greyish, covered with whitish fibres and old leaf bases. Leaves palmate, hemispherical in outline, up to a metre across (though often much less), divided into numerous narrow lanceolate sections, each often split at the apex; stiff in texture, grey-green to mid-green, held erect. Male and female flowers often on separate plants; inflorescence up to 35cm long, yellowish, but often hidden amongst the leaves. Fruits produced in a dense spike, individually globose, orange or brown.
Range and habitat: One of the very few native European palms, occurring naturally near the Mediterranean in the Iberian Peninsula; also planted more widely for ornament further north, though it is frost-sensitive.

GLOSSARY

acuminate gradually tapering into a slender point
acute sharply pointed
alternate staggered singly around stem (usually leaf arrangement)
anther part of the stamen containing the pollen
appressed (adpressed) parts pressed closely together but not joined
auricles rounded lobes at the base of a leaf
axil upper angle between a stem and a leaf or bract
basic soils rich in free basic ions, eg. calcium or magnesium
berry fleshy fruit without a stony layer surrounding the seeds
bifid split deeply into two
blade expanded, flattened part of a leaf
bloom whitish or bluish covering, very easily removed (as on the outside of some grapes)
bole lower branch-free part of a trunk
bract scale-like or leaf-like structure, from the axil of which an inflorescence or part of an inflorescence emerges
bracteole scale-like or leaf-like structure, from the axil of which a single flower emerges
bud developing shoot or flower, often protected by scales and the growth suspended during unfavourable conditions
burr lumpy outgrowth from a trunk, often covered with sprouting shoots
buttressed base of the trunk surrounded by tapering flanges or ridges
calyx sepals of a flower considered as a whole
catkin elongated, crowded inflorescence of inconspicuous, wind-pollinated flowers
ciliate margin surrounded by regularly projecting hairs
columnar narrow, almost parallel-sided crown
compound leaf made up of several distinct leaflets
cone inflorescence of a conifer, often woody and conical, composed of scales and bract
coniferous cone-bearing
coppiced cut-down regularly to the base, yielding long poles
cordate heart-shaped; often restricted to the base of a rounded lobe either side of the stalk
corolla petals of a flower considered as a whole
corymb short, broad and more or less flat-topped inflorescence, developing like a raceme
crenate margin with shallow, rounded teeth
cuneate wedge-shaped or tapering leaf-base
cyme more or less flat-topped inflorescence, each growing point terminated by a flower
deciduous dropping off; usually referring to leaves which fall in autumn
decurrent the base continued down the stem as a wing
deflexed bent sharply downwards
dentate margin with sharp teeth
digitate leaflets spreading like the fingers of a hand; palmate
dioecious with separate male and female flowers borne on different plants
drupe fleshy fruit with the seed(s) surrounded by a stony layer
elliptic outline, widest at the middle, rounded and narrowed towards each end
endemic native to a restricted region, usually a single country or smaller area
entire margin unbroken by teeth or lobes
fastigiate branches more or less upright (as in Lombardy Poplar)
filament part of the stamen, the stalk supporting the anther
filiform thread-like; long and very slender
fluted with deep vertical grooves
fruit ripe seeds and surrounding structures, either fleshy or dry
glaucous covered with a bluish or whitish layer
hermaphrodite flowers possessing both functional male and female parts

hispid covered with rather long, stiff bristly hairs

hybrid a plant originating from the fertilization of one species by another

inflorescence flower cluster including the stem bearing flowers and bracts

involucre jointed bracts, usually surrounding the base of a short dense inflorescence

lanceolate lance-shaped in outline; widest below the middle, about 3 times as long as wide

legume a dry fruit splitting along its length above and below to release its seeds

linear narrow and more or less parallel-sided

maquis thicket of tall shrubs and scattered trees, characteristic of countries bordering the Mediterranean

midrib central or main vein of a leaf

monoecious with separate male and female flowers, both on the same plant

mucronate narrowing abruptly into a small, sharp point

nectary nectar-secreting gland usually within a flower

node point on a stem where a leaf or leaves arise

obtuse blunt

opposite in pairs at the same level on the stem (usually leaf arrangement)

orbicular (in outline) rounded

ovate outline, widest below the middle, rounded towards each end

ovoid solid body, widest below the middle, ovate in cross-section

palmate leaf with more than 3 leaflets arising from the same point

panicle branched inflorescence with each branch developing like a raceme

pedicel stalk of a flower

peduncle stalk of an inflorescence or group of flowers within an inflorescence

perianth sepals and petals together

petiole stalk of a leaf

phyllode flattened, leaf-like petiole with no blade (as in Acacia)

pinnate compound leaf with many leaflets arranged either side of a central stalk (rachis)

pinnatifid leaf cut into lobes either side of central intact region

pollard tree cut back repeatedly to 2-3m above the ground

procumbent trailing; lying near to the ground

pubescent covered with short, rather soft hairs

raceme an inflorescence, usually elongated, which continually adds new, stalked flowers to the tip; the oldest flowers are thus at the base

rachis stem-like axis bearing leaflets or flowers

recurved curved backwards

reflexed bent sharply backwards

revolute curved underneath (usually leaf-margins)

sessile stalkless

simple leaf not divided into leaflets

sinuate margin wavy when viewed from above

spathe bract-like or petal-like sheath enclosing an inflorescence

spike raceme-like inflorescence with stalkless flowers

stamen male reproductive organ of a flower, consisting of anther and filament

stigma surface receptive to pollen; part of the female reproductive organs of a flower

stipule appendage at base of petiole, either scale-like or leaf-like

style part of the female reproductive organs of a flower, connecting the stigma to the ovary

subalpine at the limits of the tree-line

sucker shoots arising directly from a root, often away from the main trunk

terminal at the end or tip, usually of a branch

tomentose densely covered with rather short, soft hairs

truncate with a squarish, transverse tip

tubercle a short, blunt, smooth projection

umbel inflorescence with all the stalks arising from the same point

viscid sticky, glutinous

INDEX

158

ACKNOWLEDGEMENTS

160   Majority of the artworks are by Ian Garrard, with David More (*Salix*) and
Tim Hayward (some of the conifers). Artworks on page 143 bottom and 148
top are by Roger Gorringe.
All photographs supplied by Bob Gibbons and Natural Image.